FOOD

The Key Concepts

ISSN 1747-6550

The series aims to cover the core disciplines and the key cross-disciplinary ideas across the Humanities and Social Sciences. Each book isolates the key concepts to map out the theoretical terrain across a specific subject or idea. Designed specifically for student readers, each book in the series includes boxed case material, summary chapter bullet points, annotated guides to further reading and questions for essays and class discussion

Film: The Key Concepts
Nitzan Ben-Shaul

Globalization: The Key Concepts
Thomas Hylland Eriksen

Food: The Key Concepts
Warren Belasco

Technoculture: The Key Concepts
Debra Benita Shaw

The Body: The Key Concepts
Lisa Blackman

New Media: The Key Concepts
Nicholas Gane and David Beer

FOOD
The Key Concepts

Warren Belasco

BERG
Oxford • New York

English edition
First published in 2008 by
Berg
Editorial offices:
First Floor, Angel Court, 81 St Clements Street, Oxford OX4 1AW, UK
175 Fifth Avenue, New York, NY 10010, USA

Berg is the imprint of Oxford International Publishers Ltd.

Library of Congress Cataloging-in-Publication Data

Belasco, Warren James.
    Food : the key concepts / Warren Belasco.
        p. cm.—(The key concepts, ISSN 1747-6550)
    Includes bibliographical references and index.
    ISBN-13: 978-1-84520-672-7 (cloth)
    ISBN-10: 1-84520-672-X (cloth)
    ISBN-13: 978-1-84520-673-4 (paper)
    ISBN-10: 1-84520-673-8 (paper)
    1. Food. 2. Food—Social aspects. 3. Food habits. I. Title.

    TX353.B445 2008
    641.3—dc22

                                                            2008024617

British Library Cataloguing-in-Publication Data

A catalogue record for this book is available from the British Library.

ISBN 978 1 84520 672 7 (Cloth)
        978 1 84520 673 4 (Paper)

Typeset by JS Typesetting Ltd, Porthcawl, Mid Glamorgan
Printed in the United Kingdom by Biddles Ltd, King's Lynn

www.bergpublishers.com

This book is dedicated to my students at the University of Maryland Baltimore County and to my colleagues at the Association for the Study of Food and Society.

CONTENTS

OVERVIEW

There is nothing more basic than food. Food is the first of the essentials of life, our biggest industry, our most frequently indulged pleasure, and perhaps the greatest cause of disease and death. Despite its importance, food is often taken for granted, especially by academics, who have long considered food matters to be too coarse for scholarly attention. But the field of food studies has expanded tremendously in recent years, and many colleges and universities are now offering food-related courses designed for undergraduates in liberal arts programs.

This book offers an interdisciplinary introduction to the study of food. It opens with a brief analysis of why food has been ignored by scholars for so long. Then it offers a graphic way of understanding and thinking about how people decide what to eat. Food choices are the result of a complex negotiation among three competing considerations: the consumer's identity (social and personal), matters of convenience (price, skill, availability), and a sense of responsibility (an awareness of the consequences of what we eat). In separate chapters we look at each of these considerations. For identity we examine the psychological, cultural, and demographic determinants of what and how we eat. Since many people have very conflicted feelings about food, we devote space to how our divided identities may be represented in popular music, literature, and film. Then we look at convenience, which is provided, for profit, by the global food industry, the world's largest industry. Next, in the hopes of being responsible consumers, we examine some of the medical, political, and environmental costs of our modern feast. Finally, mindful of growing world population and diminishing resources, we examine two very different scenarios for feeding the future, the technological fix, which pins its hope on continued scientific breakthroughs, and the anthropological fix, which hopes to change human expectations and behaviors.

1 WHY STUDY FOOD?

Tell me what you eat and I will tell you what you are.

Jean Anthelme Brillat-Savarin (1755–1826)

What is food to one man may be fierce poison to others.

Lucretius (99–55 BCE)

History celebrates the battlefields whereon we meet our death, but scorns to speak of the plowed fields whereby we thrive; it knows the names of the King's bastards, but cannot tell us the origin of wheat. That is the way of human folly.

Jean Henry Fabre (1825–1915)

Welcome to food studies! Food is the first of the essentials of life, the world's largest industry, our most frequently indulged pleasure, the core of our most intimate social relationships. It's very hard to imagine a positive social experience that does not involve the sharing of food – whether a simple cup of tea with an acquaintance, a lunchtime "bite" with colleagues, or a sumptuous lobster dinner with a lover. On a broader level, civilization itself is impossible without food: with the invention of agriculture some ten thousand years ago came city states and empires, art, music, and organized warfare. Agriculture remade the world, both physically and culturally, transforming landscapes and geography, subsidizing soldiers and poets, politicians and priests (Diamond 1999: 236).

For French epicure Brillat-Savarin, we are what we eat – and for Lucretius, we are what we won't eat. Our tastes are as telling as our distastes. To be a member of the Parakana people of the Amazon rain forest is to relish roasted tapir and to despise monkey meat, while the neighboring Arara feel quite the reverse (Rensberger 1991: A3). Food identifies who we are, where we came from, and what we want to be. "Food reveals our souls," sociologist Gary Alan Fine writes. "Like Marcel Proust reminiscing about a madeleine or Calvin Trillin astonished at a plate of ribs, we are entangled in our meals" (1996:1). Food is "a highly condensed social fact," anthropologist Arjun Appadurai observes, "and a marvelously plastic kind of collective representation" (1981: 494).

Food is also the object of major anxiety, for what and how we eat may be the single most important cause of disease and death. We can't live without food, but food also kills us. As psychologist Paul Rozin puts it, "Food is fundamental, fun, frightening, and far-reaching" (1999: 9–30). And probably nothing is more frightening or far-reaching than the prospect of running out of food. "A hungry stomach will not allow its owner to forget it, whatever his cares and sorrows," Homer wrote almost 3,000 years ago. Even in good times, we are not allowed to forget our deeply rooted heritage of food insecurity. "When thou hast enough," Ecclesiasticus warned, *c.*180 BCE, "remember the time of hunger." As if to take advantage of the brief break from habitual scarcity, our bodies store up fat for the next famine – hence the current obesity crisis – while our prophets warn us against complacency. For much of history the search for sufficient food drove the conquest and colonization of continents – and the enslavement or eradication of entire populations. Food matters. It has weight, and it weighs us down.

And yet, until recently scholars were amazingly reluctant to study food, especially the aspect closest to our hearts (and arteries): food consumption. To be sure, food *production* has received considerable attention in established disciplines such as economics, chemistry, agronomy, engineering, marketing, and labor relations. Scientists have long explored the negative pathologies of malnutrition, hunger, and adulteration. But when it comes to analyzing the more positive and intimate features of what, how, and why we eat, academics have been considerably more reticent. Even now, with the rising interest in food studies, a serious analysis of family dinner rituals, cookbooks, or the appeal of fast food may still evoke surprise and even scorn. "Do professors really study *that*?" your friends and family ask. "If you're going to go around telling your colleagues you are a philosopher of food," philosopher Lisa Heldke writes, "you better be prepared to develop a thick skin – and start a wisecrack collection" (2006: 202).

Why this reluctance to address the wider meaning of our food behaviors? Why is food taken for granted, at least in academia?

For one thing, intellectuals are heirs to a classical dualism that prizes mind over body. In *Cooking, Eating, Thinking*, Heldke and her colleague Deane Curtin write, "Our tradition has tended to privilege questions about the rational, the unchanging, and the eternal, and the abstract and the mental; and to denigrate questions about embodied, concrete, practical experience" (Curtin 1992: xiv). Philosopher Carolyn Korsmeyer agrees that "Taste and eating [are] tied to the necessities of existence and are thus classified as lower functions ... operating on a primitive, near instinctual level" (1999: 1). There may indeed be some archetypal, dualistic disdain for something as mundane, corporeal, even "animalistic" as eating. "Put a knife to thy throat," urges Proverbs 23:2, "if thou be a man given to appetite." "Reason should direct and appetite obey," Cicero counseled in 44 BCE (Egerton 1994: 17). "Govern thy appetite well," advised Puritan poet John Milton, "lest Sin Surprise thee, and her black attendant Death" (Egerton 1994: 18). To some extent, we may still live with the prejudices of the nineteenth century, which gave birth to so many modern institutions, ranging from research universities to dinner parties. Genteel Victorians constructed such elaborate dining rituals partly because they harbored a deep suspicion of eating, which – like sex – they viewed as basically uncivilized. The novelist Joyce Carol Oates characterizes that attitude nicely: "Civilization is a multiplicity of strategies, dazzling as precious gems inlaid in a golden crown, to obscure from human beings the sound of, the terrible meaning of, their jaws grinding. The meaning of man's place in the food cycle that, by way of our imaginations, we had imagined might not apply to us" (1993: 25). In other words, food is gross.

Food scholarship has also been hindered by another Victorian relic, the "separate spheres" – the idealized bourgeois division between the private female sphere of *consumption* and the more public male sphere of *production*. While the concept did not reflect the daily realities for most women – to this day women are major food producers across the globe – the ideological polarization certainly influenced the development of middle-class academia, for it effectively segregated women professionals in less valued "domestic" disciplines, particularly dietetics, home economics, social work, and nutrition education (along with elementary school teaching, nursing, and library science). Conversely, the male-dominated realms of industrial agriculture, food technology, mass retailing, and corporate management *have* generally received more public respect and academic prestige.

This institutionalized bias delayed serious attention to food even after the women's movement obliterated the separate spheres. While more women began to enter all fields of academia in the 1960s, it took several decades before scholars could begin to consider the traditional female ghetto of domesticity without Victorian-era blinders and prejudices, and even today, feminists who do treasure their cooking heritage and skills may risk the hostility of colleagues who feel that women should move on to more "serious" pursuits. In recent years there have been significant and largely sympathetic reappraisals of women's food work (e.g., Strasser 1982, Cowan 1983, Shapiro 1986, 2004, DeVault 1991, Mennell et al. 1992, Avakian 1997), but the identification of food with oppression still slants the scholarship – as evidenced, perhaps, by the fact that there may be more research devoted to women's eating disorders than to women's positive connections to food.

The association of cooking with women's enslavement leads to another major reason for food's relative invisibility: technological utopianism. For millennia food *has* meant unrelenting drudgery, not just for cooks, but also for all food workers – farmers, field laborers, butchers, grocers, clerks, servers, and so on. Since at least the nineteenth century many reformers have attempted, in a sense, to "disappear" food, to make it less visible and less central as a burden or concern. Progressives applauded the modern economic shift from messy food production to automated manufacturing and white collar office jobs. Feminist utopians embraced almost any idea that would get food out of the home and thus free up women: the meal in a pill, foods synthesized from coal, centralized kitchens, and "self-service" electric appliances and convenience foods. For example, in 1870, novelist Annie Denton Cridge dreamed of a large, mechanized cooking establishment that, by feeding an eighth of Philadelphia's population at one seating, would give housewives time to read, think, and discuss big ideas – and all at a cost lower "than when every house had its little, selfish, dirty kitchen" (Belasco 2006a: 110). Similarly, farmer-utopians dreamed of push-button, fully automated factory farms as a way to save their children from back-breaking labor and rural isolation. Today we can recognize that those dreams came true; sort of. Whereas once most people were farmers, now a relative handful of highly mechanized farmers grow almost all our food, and in providing over 50 million meals a day, McDonald's comes very close to Cridge's "one big kitchen" vision. But the result has been further distancing from the traditional rituals, sensibilities, and practices of food production – as well as some negative consequences for our health and environment.

Even more important in distancing us from nature and tradition have been the efforts of the food industry to obscure and mystify the links between the farm and the dinner table. While these efforts were stepped up in mid-nineteenth century (re-flected in the above-mentioned, gendered separation of production from consump-tion), they date at least as far back as the first global food conglomerate, the East India Company, which was dedicated to bringing exotic foodstuffs to European dining rooms and whose annual report in 1701 observed, "We taste the spices of Arabia yet never feel the scorching sun which brings them forth."[1] In other words, this food company was rather proud that thanks to its noble service in distant lands, affluent consumers did not have to experience the strenuous and often violent production processes by which their sausage got peppered or their tea sweetened. Perhaps the most vivid recent example of how we no longer have to feel the "scorching sun" of food production is the meat-packing industry, whose main thrust over 150 years has been to insulate consumers from any contact with the disassembly of warm-blooded mammals into refrigerated, plastic-wrapped chops and patties. "Forget the pig as an animal," a modern livestock management journal advises. "Treat him just like a machine in a factory" (Byrnes 1976: 30). In his environmental history of Chicago, *Nature's Metropolis*, William Cronon writes that the meat-packing industry of the late nineteenth century actively encouraged such "forgetfulness." "In the packers' world it was easy not to remember that eating was a moral act inexorably bound to killing" (Cronon 1991: 256).

By the 1920s the relationship between supplier and customer, plow and plate, was largely anonymous, as noted by agricultural geneticist Edward East: "Today [1924] one sits down to breakfast, spreads out a napkin of Irish linen, opens the meal with a banana from Central America, follows with a cereal of Minnesota sweetened with the product of Cuban cane, and ends with a Montana lamb chop and cup of Brazilian coffee. Our daily life is a trip around the world, yet the wonder of it gives us not a single thrill. We are oblivious" (East 1924: 64). If consumers in the 1920s were already complacent about what East called the "globe-girdling" food supply system, they are even more "oblivious" now, when the "forgetfulness" applies not just to spices, sugar, or meat, but to virtually everything we consume: tomatoes, bread, pasta, shrimp, apple juice, grapes, cornflakes, and so on. Food is so vague in our culture in part because, thanks to processing, packaging, and marketing, it *is* an abstraction – an almost infinite set of variations on a theme of corn, which, Michael Pollan demonstrates, is the basis of so many modern foodstuffs, from Big Macs to Twinkies (Pollan 2006: 15–31). According to farmer-poet Wendell Berry, the ideal corporate customer today is the "industrial eater ... who does not know that eating is an agricultural act, who no longer knows or imagines the connections between eating and the land, and who is therefore necessarily passive and uncritical" (1989: 126). And furthering the critical challenges to those attempting to uncover the complex commodity chains connecting field and fork is the fact that people may not eat as regularly or as socially as they used to. Given that modern meals themselves are so ephemeral, it is not surprising that it takes some effort to see food as a subject worthy of serious social analysis.

Yet, despite these difficulties and delays, there is no question that more people are studying food than ever before. While it may be premature to announce the birth of a new discipline of food studies, signs of increased activity are everywhere. In addition to the food-related papers now presented regularly at mainstream academic conventions, there have been a number of major international conferences devoted entirely to food, and these have, in turn resulted in published collections (e.g., Lentz 1999, Grew 1999, Mack 1999, Dietler and Hayden 2000, Belasco and Scranton 2002, Jacobs and Scholliers 2003). New academic journals are appearing, culinary history societies are mushrooming, and publishers are announcing food series. There is also a lively market for food-related memoirs, essays, and annotated historical recipes. Serious analyses of the food system by Michael Pollan, Eric Schlosser, Laura Shapiro, and Marion Nestle straddle both "trade" (general) and textbook audiences. There are dozens of excellent websites devoted to the disciplined exploration of foodways, not to mention the thousands of sites dedicated to cooking, gastronomy, nutrition, and restaurant reviews. As hundreds of professors offer undergraduate food-related courses, several universities have established food studies concentrations and degrees, while other students seek to "do food" within conventional disciplines such as history, anthropology, and literary studies.

Trend-watchers might ask, why now? In part, scholarship is following wider urban middle-class culture, which, since the 1970s, has become much more interested in food-related matters of taste, craft, authenticity, status, and health. Food scholars belong to the same affluent social class that has fueled an unprecedented expansion and elaboration of restaurant and supermarket options, and that well-educated, trend-conscious public is literally hungry for analysis and perspective. Enthusiastic journalists and documentary filmmakers popularize the new work of food scholars. Socially conscious food professionals – chefs, managers, cookbook writers, etc. – also mingle and exchange ideas with food professors. Furthermore, as the world seems to spin helplessly from one major political crisis to another, large segments of the public look for ways to assert some control over their lives – and watching what you eat may be one such way to feel in charge of your destiny. Along these lines, the academic left has found food studies to be a fertile base for activist analysis of hunger, inequality, neo-colonialism, corporate accountability, biotechnology, globalization, and ecological sustainability. These concerns underlie much of the food scholarship today and animate many new food studies courses, where students often attempt to recover and illuminate the invisible links in the global food chain. Finding out where our food comes from is an important step toward taking responsibility for our food's true *cost*, which Henry David Thoreau defined as "the amount of life exchanged for it, immediately or in the long run" (Orr 1994: 172).

So while food studies is now "respectable," it is also inherently subversive. To study food often requires us to cross disciplinary boundaries and to ask inconvenient questions. The food supply belongs to us all, yet in the past 100 years or so we have delegated the responsibility for understanding and controlling just about every step of the metabolic process to highly credentialed experts. These specialists have managed to mystify food so thoroughly that many people simply throw up their hands in justifiable confusion when it comes to understanding essential issues of health, agriculture, and business, not to mention cooking and taste. Michael Pollan writes, "Somehow this most elemental of activities – figuring out what to eat – has come to require a remarkable amount of expert help." Decrying "our national eating disorder," Pollan asks, "How did we ever get to a point where we need investigative journalists to tell us where our food comes from and nutritionists to determine the dinner menu?" (Pollan 2006: 1). Yet all too often the experts have led us astray – as for example period after the Second World War, when specialists with endowed chairs at elite universities assured us that the first modern pesticide, DDT, was perfectly safe, that the Basic Four Food Groups constituted the best diet, and that in the near future we'd be defeating world hunger with steaks made from algae, yeast, and coal dust.

Specialists are useful to have around, of course, since modern life is far too complex for us to understand everything. But the problem with relying entirely on specialists is that sometimes they're wrong. Or worse, they tend to disagree. So to help us sort out the issues and gain some needed perspective, we need generalists – people with a decent grounding in science *and* poetry, agriculture *and* philosophy, who are not afraid to question assumptions, values, and methods. True, we may not understand all the biochemistry involved in nutrition, but we can speculate about why certain foods "taste good" at particular times and to particular people. We may not be able to explain why one pesticide works better on mites than another, but we can still ask why farm workers' children seem especially cancer-prone. We may not fully understand how genetic engineering works, but we still can wonder whether it is necessary in the first place. Such issues require that we think about matters political, historical, economic, sociocultural, and scientific *all at once.* As generalists, we study food as a *system.* Such holistic thinking actually restores our sense of power and humanity, for when it comes to eating, humans *are* generalists, i.e. omnivores.

While interdisciplinary study may entail a freewheeling crossing of disciplinary boundaries, it also requires a careful integration of themes or models on which to hang all these disparate ideas and insights. One needs to avoid the smorgasbord approach to learning – a little of this, a little of that. Or, to use another food metaphor, you can't leave a supermarket without bags to put all the groceries in, otherwise you have a big mess on the floor. The inquiry needs sturdy containers in which to carry all that stuff away.

To organize our inquiry, this book begins with the single question, "So what's for dinner?" Deciding what to eat may not be as simple as it sounds, for "Since Eve ate apples," Bryon quipped, "much depends on dinner." Eating entails a host of personal, social, and even global factors that, in their entirety, add up to a complex *food system.* To sort out these variables, imagine a triangle with one point at the top and two on the bottom. Focus first on the baseline: call the left point "Identity," the right "Convenience." And call the apex "Responsibility."

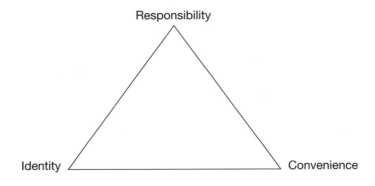

Box 1.1. So What's For Dinner?

This exercise asks you to negotiate the "culinary triangle" of contradictions. You are hosting a dinner for a very diverse group of people, including a vegetarian, a dairy farmer, a nutritionist, a hunger activist, your mother, and yourself. As a gracious host, you want to please everyone, or at the very least, you do not want to offend anyone. Everyone must eat; there cannot be any hasty, angry departures from the table. You also want to serve a meal that reflects your own tastes and values, and you don't want to spend a lot of time or money on it. What on earth can you serve? Describe the menu, taking care to show how it will appeal to each guest's sense of identity. In addition, explain how the menu is both "responsible" and "convenient."

Note: Try this exercise before you read the rest of this book and then again after you have finished it. Compare your answers.

For additional readings that analyze meals in this contemplative fashion, see: Visser 1986, Rozin 1994, Gussow 2001, Pollan 2006, and Kingsolver 2007.

For the most part, people decide what to eat based on a rough negotiation – a pushing and tugging – between the dictates of identity and convenience, with somewhat lesser guidance from the considerations of responsibility. (The triangle is thus not quite equilateral, though the moralist might wish it were so.)

"Identity" involves considerations of personal preference, pleasure, creativity, the sense of who and where you are. Identity includes factors such as taste, family and ethnic background, personal memories (the association between particular foods and past events, both good and bad). The cultural aspects of identity include widely shared values and ideas, extravagant notions about the good life, as well as a community's special food preferences and practices that distinguish it from other communities – for example, those tapir-relishing Parakana versus the tapir-hating Arara. Gender also matters considerably in many cultures, as foods are often grouped as "male" and female" – for example, steaks versus salads. Deeply rooted in childhood, tradition, and group membership, the culinary dictates of identity are hard to change, because they raise questions such as "How do I eat it?," "Should I like it?," "Is this *authentic*?," and "Is this what people like me eat?" At the identity point, food choices are expressed through rituals, etiquette, symbols, and arts. In studying food and identity (Chapters 2–3), we look at what, where, and how people eat – and *don't* eat. And we examine how they represent, play with, and think about their food.

"Convenience" encompasses variables such as price, availability, and ease of preparation, which are all related to the requirements of energy, time, labor, and skill. In other words, convenience involves concerns such as "Can I get it?," "Can I afford it?," "Can I make it?" Accounting for these all-important factors of convenience will lead us to look at the global food chain – the series of steps and processes by which food gets from farm to fork. Hence, in Chapter 4 we will examine the role of the people and institutions that make food accessible to us – e.g., farmers, migrant workers, processors, supermarkets, and restaurants. By smoothing food's flow from field to plate, for a price, the food industry sells us convenience. To be sure, there are enormous differences in the degree of convenience afforded different consumers. Some of us in the world have almost instant access to an unprecedented array of meal options, while other people's choices are severely restricted by economics, environment, and social structure. Such differences are starkly presented in *Hungry Planet*, where thirty families from all over the world are lined up separately behind a week's worth of food. Families from North America, Europe, Australia, and Kuwait are almost hidden by immense piles of plastic-wrapped "convenience foods," while people from Mali, Ecuador, and India seem much larger than the baskets of unprocessed grains and produce they consume. Somewhere in between, representing the world's "middle class," families from the Philippines, China, and Egypt stand around tables covered with raw fruits and grains as well as bottled soft drinks and bags of snacks (Menzel and D'Aluisio 2005).

And then, there's the matter of responsibility, which I put at the apex of the triangle not because it is the strongest factor but because maybe it *should* be. Responsibility entails being aware of the consequences of one's actions – both personal and social, physiological and political. It can involve short-term, acute consequences: Will this meal make me sick tomorrow? And it can involve long-term effects: Will it make me sick thirty years from now? Being responsible means being aware of one's place in the food chain – of the enormous impact we have on nature, animals, other people, and the distribution of power and resources all over the globe. It means feeling that "scorching sun" of the East India Company's Arabian enterprises; or appreciating Thoreau's "amount of life exchanged" to get your meal from farm to fork; or calculating, as the Great Law of the Iroquois Confederacy once attempted, "the impact of our decisions on the next seven generations." In eating even the simplest dish we join a chain of events linking people and places across the world and across time, too – past and future. "We are paying for the foolishness of yesterday while we shape our own tomorrow," environmentalist William Vogt wrote in 1948. "Today's white bread may force a break in the levees and flood New Orleans next spring. This year's wheat from Australia's eroding slopes may flare into a Japanese war three decades hence." Having a sense of responsibility entails both remembering how the food got to you (the past) and anticipating the consequences down the line (the future). "We must develop our sense of time and think of the availability of beefsteaks not only for this Saturday but for the Saturdays of our old age, and of our children" (Vogt 1948: 285, 63). Ultimately, assigning responsibility is a political process, for it entails sorting out the separate duties of individual consumers, food providers, and government. The poet-farmer Wendell Berry writes that "To eat responsibly is to understand and enact, as far as one can, the complex relationship" between the individual and the food system (Berry 1989: 129).

Although I have placed responsibility at the apex of my triangle, it is often the weakest of the three forces pulling at the individual food consumer. Still, many of us do want to be "conscientious consumers." "The unexamined life is not worth living," Socrates argued on behalf of acute self-consciousness. Also, knowing that "there's no free lunch," few of us want to be considered "deadbeats" – irresponsible people who skip out on the check, or worse, let our children pay our debts and then leave them worse off. "We're committing grand larceny against our children," was the charge put by environmental moralist David Brower when describing our reliance on wasteful, unsustainable resources and technologies. "Ours is a chain-letter economy, in which we pick up early handsome dividends and our children find their mailboxes empty" (McPhee 1971: 82). Chapters 5 and 6 survey some of the consequences – personal and political, immediate and distant – of our food choices and practices.

To illustrate the complexities and rewards of taking this type of comprehensive, multidisciplinary approach to food, let's think about the simple act of toasting a piece of sliced white bread. Start with identity: Where does toast fit in the morning meal rituals of certain peoples? Why have so many cultures traditionally valued processed white grains over more nutritious whole grains, while wholegrain bread is now an elite marker? Why do we like the crunchy texture ("mouth feel") of toasted foods – and is the fondness for toasted *bread* widespread or, as one encyclopedia suggests, "Anglo-bred"? (Tobias 2004: 122). Why is wheat bread the "staff" of life in some cultures, while others put rice or corn tortillas in that central position? "No foodstuff bears greater moral and philosophical burden" than bread, food writer Tom Jaine observes (1999: 97). Who invented the sandwich and what social function does it serve? Why do some cultures prefer wraps to sandwiches?

Then there are the convenience factors: Who grew, gathered, milled, and packaged the wheat? Who baked the bread? How did bread get so cheap? To turn the wheat into inexpensive sliced bread it required the coordinated efforts of numerous companies specializing in food transportation, storage, processing, and marketing, as well as many others involved in manufacturing and selling tractors, trucks, slicers, and so on. Who invented sliced bread anyway? When did store-bought white bread replace homemade whole wheat? When did they start putting vitamins back in white bread, and why? And who invented the pop-up toaster, and why?

And as for responsibility, think of toast's enormous "ecological footprint" (Wackernagel and Rees 1996). Growing that wheat helped some farmers pay their bills while also polluting their water supply with fertilizers and pesticides, eroding their soil, and, if they used irrigation, lowering their region's water table. The land used to grow the wheat had been acquired – or seized – long ago from other living creatures, human and otherwise, and converted to growing a grass that had originated as a weed in the Middle East and had been gradually domesticated and improved by 500 generations of gatherers, peasants, farmers, and, only just recently, scientists. By extending the bread's shelf life, the plastic wrapping lowered costs, raised consumer convenience, and increased profits for corporate processors, distributors, and supermarkets. That packaging also helped to put thousands of neighborhood bakers out of business. Making the plastic from petrochemicals may have helped to foul Cancer Alley in Louisiana, and if the oil came from the Middle East, may have helped to pay for the restoration of royalty in Kuwait, which was destroyed several years ago by an Iraqi army *also* financed by petrochemical bread wrappers. (Or perhaps the oil came from Venezuela, where it paid for Hugo Chavez's left-leaning reorganization of the oligarchy.) The copper in the toaster and electrical wiring may have been mined during the dictatorships of Pinochet in Chile, Mobutu in Zaire, or Chiluba in Zambia. The electricity itself probably came from a power plant burning coal, a source of black lung, acid rain, and global warming. And so on ... All of this – and much more – involved in making toast. And we have not even mentioned the butter and jam!

While the variables affecting our decision to toast bread are complex, they are relatively uncontroversial compared with the triangle of tense contradictions surrounding the decision to eat another central staple, meat.

Identity: The ability to afford meat has long served as a badge of success, health, and power, especially for men. Throughout the world, economic mobility has almost invariably meant an increase in meat consumption – a process called a "nutrition transition" (Sobal 1999: 178). Given the prestige accorded beef, particularly in the West, it is not surprising that the "cowboy" – a Spanish invention (*vaquero*) – has achieved mythical status. While some cultures accord culinary primacy to cattle, others prize pigs, sheep, poultry, fish, and rodents, and some eat no meat at all. Westerners have long denigrated vegetarian cuisines, and such prejudices have even been reflected in medical texts, as in a 1909 text: "White bread, red meat, and blue blood make the tricolor flag of conquest." "The rice-eating Hindoo and Chinese, and the potato-eating Irish are kept in subjection by the well-fed English," influential Victorian physician George Beard agreed. Conversely, vegetarians may frame meat eaters as less "civilized," as in George Bernard Shaw's famous prediction, "A hundred years hence a cultivated man will no more dream of eating flesh or smoking than he now does of living, as [Samuel] Pepys' [seventeenth century] contemporaries did, in a house with a cesspool under it." Whether staple or taboo, animal foods carry significant cultural meaning throughout the world (Belasco 2006a: 8, 10).

Convenience: Biologically, meat may be prized because it offers a compact package of nutrients. It can be relatively easy to cook, especially if it is of the well-fatted, grain-fed variety produced by the modern livestock industry. Meat production has long been the focus of many laborsaving innovations – hence the early rise of the slaughterhouse "disassembly" line, which in turn became the model for so many other mass production industries. A significant proportion – perhaps even most – of modern agricultural science is devoted to devising ever more efficient ways to grow cheap corn and soy for livestock, especially fat-marbled beef. And making this meat convenient – cheap, easy, and accessible – is also a primary goal and achievement of the fast food industry

But the responsibility considerations are enormous: acute poisoning from "dirty beef," chronic heart disease from animal fats, the possible mistreatment of animals and workers in animal factories, the immediate and long-term impact on the environment in terms of energy, groundwater pollution, soil loss, and even climate change. The resource-intensive nature of animal production has been known for centuries. William Paley's 1785 *Principles of Moral and Political Philosophy* observes: "A piece of ground capable of supplying animal food sufficient for the subsistence of ten persons would sustain, at least, the double of that number with grain, roots, and milk." In 1811, radical publisher Richard Phillips argued that British farmers could potentially feed 47 million vegetarians "in abundance," "but they sustain only twelve millions *scantily*" on animal products (Belasco 2006a: 5).

In addition there are the conflicts ensuing from differences in diet, especially meat-eaters vs. vegetarians. In Plato's *Republic,* written over 2,400 years ago, Socrates argued that because domesticated meat production required so much land, it inevitably led to territorial expansion and war with vegetarian neighbors (Adams 1992: 115). In *Guns, Germs, and Steel* Jared Diamond suggests that Eurasia – Plato's home region – was the origin of many expansionist empires precisely because it harbored such an abundance of domesticated mammals (1997: 157–175). According to medievalist Massimo Montanari, invasion of the declining, and still largely vegetarian Roman Empire by northern, meat-eating "barbarians" brought widespread deforestation and consolidated landholding to accommodate larger herds of livestock (1999: 77–78). Following the adoption of this Germanic model, environmental historian William Cronon observes, "domesticated grazing animals – and the tool which they made possible, the plow – were arguably the single most distinguishing characteristic of European agricultural practices." And after 1492 European livestock may have done more to destroy Native American ecosystems than all the invading armies combined

(1983: 128). "The introduction of livestock proved to be the greatest success story in the culinary conquest of America," Jeffrey Pilcher observes in his history of Mexican foodways. "Herds [of cattle] overran the countryside, driving Indians from their fields" (1998: 30).

Differences in gender attitudes toward meat also have had important consequences. Men have long invoked their power over women as a rationalization for having the best cuts of scarce meat, and such differences in nutrition may indeed have made men more powerful than women deprived of iron, protein, and calcium. In short, with so much at stake in our steaks, there is an almost classic conflict between the rich rewards and stark consequences of an animal-based diet. Such conflicts make for exciting drama – and interesting study.

But let us not rush to the more disturbing elements of the story. Before disenchantment comes enchantment – the almost magical ways that food reveals identity and creates relationships.

Chapter Summary

- Food matters, yet it has been little studied by academics.
- Food consumption and preparation have long been associated with women's world, and thus have been accorded less respect and attention than male activities.
- The drudgery of food production has inspired many efforts to "disappear it."
- Distancing from food production leads many modern consumers to take food for granted.
- Studying food is interdisciplinary, respectable, and subversive.
- Deciding what to eat entails a rough negotiation among considerations of identity, convenience, and responsibility.
- The food industry's primary product is convenience.
- Responsibility entails being aware of the consequences of one's actions.
- Meat has a central place in the modern diet because it is an emblem of success and power (identity), and it is relatively convenient to cook and consume. Its "consequences" are equally monumental.

2 IDENTITY: ARE WE WHAT WE EAT?

> For what is food? It is not only a collection of products that can be used for statistical or nutritional studies. It is also, and at the same time, a system of communication, a body of images, a protocol of usages, situations, and behavior.
>
> Roland Barthes (1979)

We start our inquiry, to repeat Paul Rozin (1999), with the most "fundamental" and "fun" aspects of food – the way food serves to express personal and group identities and to cement social bonds. These functions may be taken for granted in our modern world, where eating is often of the "grab and go" variety and where consumers are so removed from the complex and nearly miraculous means by which solar energy and chemical elements are transformed into "dishes," "meals," and "feasts."

It is an axiom of food studies that "dining" is much more than "feeding." While all creatures "feed," only humans "dine." As the French cultural theorist Barthes suggests above, what we consider "food" extends far beyond nutrients, calories, and minerals. A meal is much more than the sum of its parts, for it encompasses what Barthes calls "a system of communication, a body of images, a protocol of usages, situations, and behavior" (Barthes 1979: 166–173). People use food to "speak" with each other, to establish rules of behavior ("protocols"), and to reveal, as Brillat-Savarin said, "what you are."

CUISINE

One way to understand the expressive and normative functions of food is through the key concept of "cuisine." In popular language the term "cuisine" is often reserved for high-class, elite, or "gourmet" food. But here, following anthropologists Peter Farb and George Armelagos (1980: 190–98), we take a more expansive view to suggest that *all* groups have an identifiable "cuisine," a shared set of "protocols," usages, communications, behaviors, etc. (A similar meaning applies to the word "culture," which extends beyond just Shakespeare, operas, and fine art to encompass a common set of ideas, images and values that express and influence how group members think, feel and act.) Cuisine and culture vary widely from group to group. While the human race as a whole has tried to eat just about everything on the planet and may thus be considered to be omnivorous, specific groups are quite picky. That is, within individual cuisines certain foods are considered "good to eat" and "good to think" (yum) while others are considered "inedible" or "disgusting" (yuck).

Farb and Armelagos liken a cuisine to a culture's language – a system of communication that is inculcated from birth, if not before, and is hard to change or learn once you are grown. Even if you migrate elsewhere, you will likely retain the "accent" of your native cuisine. A similar concept is that of the "food voice," which may range, according to Annie Hauck-Lawson, from "whispers" and "utterances" to "shouts" and "choruses" (2004: 24). As with all vocalizations, some national cuisines speak more loudly than others; while Irish or Scandinavian cuisines may tend to be somewhat muted in range and resonance, Italian and Chinese are almost operatic in dramatic intensity. Similarly an individual cook's food voice may be more or less eloquent and evocative. Another way to imagine these differences in cuisine is to think in terms of menus: some restaurants (cuisines) offer long and challenging lists of complex dishes, while others stick to a short "McMenu."

Farb and Armelagos, along with culinary historian Elisabeth Rozin (1982), suggest that a group's cuisine has four main elements.

First, each cuisine prioritizes a limited set of "basic foods," the primary "edibles" selected from a broader environment of potential foods. These selections are based on a mix of convenience, identity, and responsibility considerations. As Rozin puts it, "The general rule seems to be that everyone eats some things, but no one eats all things, and the basis for the selection of foods by a culture is dependent on a wide variety of factors: availability, ease of production, nutritional costs and benefits, custom, palatability, religious or social sanction." Other analysts call these most highly prized staples "core" foods or "cultural super foods." In a seminal analysis of migrant Mexican American food practices, anthropologist Brett Williams (1984) distinguishes tortillas (the simple, daily staples) from tamales (the time-consuming dishes reserved for special occasions). "Basic foods" range from meat and potatoes in Nebraska, to stew and fufu (porridge) in West Africa, to rice and soy in East Asia, and, yes, to tortillas and beans in Central America.

Second, specific cuisines favor a distinct manner of preparing food. Rozin identifies several main "manipulative techniques," including particulation (cutting, slicing, mincing into smaller sizes), incorporation (mixing two substances to yield a third, such as the combination of water and milled grain to produce dough),

Box 2.1. A Holiday Meal

It is within the family that we do most of our eating. Through a complex set of domestic interactions, we learn how to eat, shop, and cook; what to like, and what to dislike. We also observe rituals, celebrate holidays, and create new traditions while discarding others. In this exercise you will apply the concept of "cuisine" to describe and interpret a festive family dinner ritual — i.e., a special meal that is planned, periodic, predictable, and especially loaded with *meaning*.

1. Introduction: What sort of meal is this and who's coming? That is, give the overall setting: type of event, time, place, personnel.
2. Food choices: Give a typical menu and tell me where the basic foods come from. Note prevailing color patterns, shapes, textures, flavor principles. Whose food preferences prevail when it comes to planning the meal? How do these foods compare with those used in daily meals?
3. Manner of preparation: Who acquires the food? Who prepares it? Describe any specialization or division of labor. Describe the main manipulative techniques. Which dishes are made "from scratch"? From a box? Where did the recipes come from? Who cleans up? Evaluate and rate the kitchen work as a theatrical performance. (Is it a good "show"?)
4. Rules for consumption: How is the meal performed? Describe:
   — Time and length of meal.
   — Meal site (dining room, kitchen, family room, etc.).
   — Types of utensils, dishes, napkins.
   — Seating arrangements at the table.
   — Serving procedures.
   — Aesthetic arrangement of food on the table and on the plate.
   — Appropriate dress.
   — Appropriate conversation topics.
   — Procedures for departure from the table.
   — Post-meal rituals.
   — Other relevant "table manners."
   — Family idiosyncrasies.
   — Comparison with ordinary daily meals.

Further reading on meal rituals: Douglas 1975, Etzioni 2004, Visser 1991, Dietler and Hayden 2001, Jacobs and Scholliers 2003, Albala 2007, Pitts et al. 2007.

marination, application of dry or wet heat, dry curing, frying, and fermentation. Such techniques vary widely depending on the energy, time, skill, personnel and technologies available in individual kitchens. Noting how convenience and identity factors interact, Farb and Armelagos detect some "wisdom of cuisine" in the way that some groups ingeniously exploit scarce energy resources – such as low-fat stir-frying in Asia and quick fermentation in hot and humid West Africa – but such "wisdom" is less obvious when it comes to the far less efficient microwaving of elaborately packaged "convenience foods" or the grilling of hamburgers produced in energy-intensive animal factories. Still, it is fair to say that humans have been very creative in devising numerous ways to transform the "raw" into the "cooked," and learning about such techniques is one of the delights of food studies – and a major appeal of cooking shows on television.

Cuisines are also distinguished by their "flavor principles" – a distinctive way of seasoning dishes. These unique flavoring combinations serve as important group "markers." For example, culinary identity in parts of China may be expressed through the combination of soy sauce, garlic, ginger, and sesame oil, while a mix of garlic, tomato, and olive oil may signal "southern Italian," and chili, cumin, garlic, and tomato may communicate "Mexican." To be sure, regional and personal variations in seasoning are extensive, so one must be wary of over-generalizing – except perhaps if you are a mass-marketer selling stereotypical "ethnic foods" such as tacos, spaghetti sauce, or egg rolls (Belasco 1987).

Cuisines also prescribe the way food is to be eaten – a set of "manners," codes of etiquette, Barthes's "protocols." These socially transmitted norms of behavior establish the boundaries of acceptability. As the Victorians were particularly concerned about separating the "civilized" from the "savage," their rules were particularly complex. As one 1879 rulebook put it, etiquette "is the barrier which society draws around itself, a shield against the intrusion of the impertinent, the improper, and the vulgar." But all cultures have their rules, culinary historian Margaret Visser notes, for "without them food would be hogged by the physically powerful, civility in general would decline, and eventually society would break down altogether. Furthermore the specific fashion in which a culture manages eating helps to express, identify, and dramatize that society's ideals and aesthetic style" (Visser 2003: 586, 588).

Here again notions and practices vary greatly, including the number of meals to be eaten per day, when, where, with what utensils, and with whom. Some cuisines favor pickled fish and rice for breakfast, others flaked grains with cold, pasteurized cow's milk. Some dine on the floor, others at tall tables. Some use the fingers of one hand, others use sticks, while others use prongs. Some compliment the cook with gentle burps while others finds such expressions to be unimaginably crude. In some societies women eat after men, in others at the same time but in another room.

Hierarchies of power and preference may also be expressed by the seating of guests, especially how close to the host and on which hand. Within cuisines the rules may also change depending on the importance or "weight" of a particular dining event. A casual "drink" with acquaintances entails quite a different set of protocols from a formal banquet with one's boss or in-laws. An afternoon snack may have fewer protocols than a wedding. And even weddings are celebrated with varying degrees of culinary attention. A nuptial dinner in Connecticut may take years to plan and cost a year's pay (or more), while in parts of Mali a bride may not know whom she is marrying until her wedding day, and no food at all will be served at the ensuing party (Menzel and D'Aluisio 2005: 216).

Generally, however, pleasant social gatherings involve food consumption, whereas food is usually prohibited in less friendly venues, such as traffic court, or, in keeping with the classic mind–body distinction, in many libraries and classrooms. While banning food from library stacks makes some sense, for this does protect the books, the general proscription on eating in class seems unfortunate, especially if the learning involves teamwork. According to the concept of *commensality*, sharing food has almost magical properties in its ability to turn self-seeking individuals into a collaborative group. Take, for example, the classic French folk tale, "Stone Soup." The story has many variants, but the general theme is food's transformative properties. In the midst of prolonged war, hungry soldiers stumble on a small village whose self-protective inhabitants, in standard peasant practice, have hidden all the edibles. (Potatoes in particular were especially useful for this, as they could be kept in the ground until needed.) At first the residents hesitate to share any food with the soldiers. But when the visitors state that all they need is a large stone and a pot, the peasants become curious and gather around to watch them boil the rock. Soon a soldier suggests that, while stone soup is wonderful, it would be better with a potato, and one intrigued peasant volunteers one of his own. The same happens when the cook muses about a carrot. Then meat, wine, tables, music, and so on follow. Soon the whole village is engaged in a hearty feast and the soldiers are invited to sleep in the mayor's best bed. Upon their departure the next day, the peasants send them off with many thanks, "for we shall never go hungry now that you have taught us how to make soup from stones!" (Brown 1947). The message: Sharing food makes us wiser, better people. This belief is also expressed in the Latin-based words "company" and "companions": the people with whom one shares bread.

Still, despite this general principle, an even rudimentary understanding of cultural anthropology or history suggests that many of the practices that we take to be timeless and universal are in fact highly variable and only recently "constructed." Widespread Western use of forks is relatively recent; King Louis XIV of France considered them "unmanly," while American Puritan settlers supposedly denounced them as devilish

(Young 2004: 437). It was not until the mid-eighteenth century that at least half of New Englanders owned forks – and these were mostly of the "middling" classes (McWilliams 2005: 216). Many of us consider the well-mannered and elaborately equipped "family meal" to be sacrosanct, "traditional," and now endangered, yet here again we can date such rituals back only to the nineteenth century, and even then inconvenient work routines, cramped space, and limited tools kept many working families from dining together (Grover 1987, Turner 2006). Solitary eating is not a purely modern invention or affliction (Mayo 2007). Conversely, despite much moralizing to the contrary, modern families may be eating together more often than assumed, although the "rules for consumption" of a takeout pizza in front of the television may be quite a bit more informal and ad hoc than those idealized by Victorian gentry or depicted by Norman Rockwell.

To these four main characteristics of cuisine may be added a fifth: a distinctive infrastructure, or "food chain," by which a group's food moves from farm to fork. Some societies have very simple infrastructures – what's raised in adjacent fields is transported a short distance to a family's home, with only a few products supplied through the nearby market. Modern cuisines, on the other hand, have highly segmented and extended food chains in which a single bite may move thousands of "food miles," with many opportunities for "adding value" (profit) by countless middlemen before it finally reaches the mouth. Thus do a few cents' worth of wheat and sweeteners become a US$4 box of Frosted Flakes. The modern food supply chain includes not only the familiar farms, truckers, factories, restaurants, and supermarkets, but also research universities, government agencies (both civilian and military), agribusiness suppliers, and oil companies. If we add up all the institutions that help to feed Americans, at least twenty percent of the US workforce is involved, with an annual bill of at least US$1 trillion. Even so, despite the huge price tag, stocking the modern commissary may occupy a much smaller percentage of the population than in a society where food travels just a few steps from the back plot. Since such complex supply chains have made modern food considerably more convenient; we will examine them more closely in Chapter 4, while Chapters 5 and 6 will ponder their vast ecological, economic, and political consequences.

To illustrate these concepts, we may inquire, "What's *American* cuisine?" The question is quite complicated, as many serious scholars debate whether Americans even *have* a cuisine, or they doubt that the term is really applicable to an entity as uniquely amorphous as the USA (Mintz: 1996). Others use their answer as an opportunity to criticize "tasteless" American mass culture. When I ask undergraduate liberal arts students this question (as I do every year), I get certain predictable phrases: fast, fried, super-sized, salty, greasy, bland, and mass-marketed. Mindful of America's multicultural heritage and nature, others will cite "diversity," "the melting pot," and "creolization." Immigration historian Donna Gabaccia writes, "The American penchant to experiment with foods, to combine and mix the foods of many cultural traditions into blended gumbos or stews, and to create 'smorgasbords' is scarcely new but is rather a recurring theme in our history as eaters" (1998: 3). Yet such celebrations of American culinary complexity are relatively recent. For a long time there *was* what might be considered a *dominant* cuisine of North America, the food beliefs and practices most associated with the heritage of British America's earliest ruling class. This hegemonic cuisine governed American cookbooks, etiquette manuals, menus, and supply chains well past the middle of the twentieth century. So what follows may be considered a rough sketch of "American cuisine" *c.* 1960. I write mostly in the past tense, as our understanding of what is "American" has become considerably more contested in the past few decades, although much of this still applies to broad segments of what is sometimes called Middle America (Levenstein 1988, Pillsbury 1998, McWilliams 2005).

Basic Foods: In keeping with its Anglo- heritage, American cuisine put meat, especially beef, at the center of the plate, while "starch" was considered to be a wrapper or side dish and vegetables mere embroidery. The Spanish, too, prioritized meat and wheat, pushing indigenous maize, legumes, and produce to the side (Pilcher 1998). As meat and dairy products have long been cheaper and more available in America than elsewhere – thanks in large part to the huge government subsidies devoted to replacing native grasses, buffalo, and Indians with corn, cows, and cowboys – almost all immigrants have added prodigious amounts of animal foods to their Old World cuisines (Diner 2001). Ratifying and rationalizing their tastes, Americans still consider animal protein to be essential for proper nutrition. Reflecting the New Nutrition of the early twentieth century (Levenstein 1988) vegetables became "good for you" but were considered "boring" and not "filling," except perhaps for salads, corn, and potatoes slathered in animal fats. At the high point of WASP hegemony, the emblematic vegetable dish was a mixture of finely chopped raw vegetables molded – indeed imprisoned – in plain gelatin, a byproduct of the slaughterhouses. According to food writer Laura Shapiro, this "perfection salad," was "the very image of a salad at last in control of itself" (1986: 100). This compulsion to encase the vegetable within the animal endures in the Jell-O cookery that is the pride of much Middle American cuisine. Conversely, the belief that a grain-centered diet is inadequate and perhaps even dangerous persists in the belief that "starches" are fattening, and thus out of control.

Flavor Principles: Genteel Americans long disdained certain strong spices – especially garlic and hot peppers – perhaps because they were too closely associated with lower-class immigrants, or perhaps because, Farb and Armelagos speculate, blandness served as a common denominator in a highly pluralistic society. Here again, the British heritage mattered, for eighteenth-century French philosopher Voltaire allegedly sniped that England was a nation of "sixty different religions but only one sauce" (Egerton 1994: 44). Valuing "honesty" and "sincerity," colonists suspected sauces of inherent elitism, especially of the upper-class French variety (Kaufman 2004: 403). To be sure American gentry loved a crude version of French food even in the early republican period, and the taste for complex spices has expanded much in recent years. Even so, the process of "Americanization" today still resembles the way Victorians absorbed a few "foreign foods," such as "Hindoo" curries and Chinese "chop suey" – by "blunting the flavors and dismantling the complications" (Shapiro 1986: 213).

In keeping with their traditional wariness of Old World cuisines, modernistic Americans were quick to accept canned, frozen, and otherwise processed foods, but only by being convinced through advertising and branding that they were somehow "fresh" and "natural." (In this way the modern was reconciled with the traditional.) Among the main criteria for "freshness" in North American cuisine:

- Packaged bread should be "soft." Firm, chewy bread was considered "stale" (unless toasted).
- Vegetables must have certain predictable colors, generally "bright." Tomatoes, strawberries, and apples must be a certain shade of red; carrots and oranges, orange; string beans, peppers, and squash, green; bananas, yellow. Similar color standards applied to animal foods, e.g., yellow butter, margarine, and chicken, "red" meat. To achieve these colors, certain genetic strains were favored, and as a last resort dyes and waxes might be added. (Here again, modernistic means were employed to achieve "traditional" ends.)
- Sweetness was equated with freshness, hence the addition of sugar to most processed foods. And extra sodium perked up tired canned and frozen foods, restoring some of the "natural" flavor lost somewhere along the extended food chain.
- For drinks: the colder the better. "Keep it cold, keep it fresh." Room-temperature ales might be considered highly drinkable in Britain but were considered "flat" in America. Only an extravagantly affluent society could afford such widespread and extreme refrigeration. (Convenience thus reinforced taste.) Cheap refrigeration also shaped the American preference for dry-aged refrigerated beef – thought to be more "tender" (or at least softer) than freshly killed meat (Pilcher 2006: 10–11). At the same time, reflecting the same abundance of fossil fuels, "hot" meals had to be *really* hot – no lukewarm street foods here. Coffee and tea had to be either "iced" or boiled.
- Given the growing distance between real farms and urban markets, consumers were easily assured of a product's freshness by advertisements that depicted

stereotypical, Disneyesque farm scenes of ruggedly hearty family farmers, well-groomed, pest-free fields, and contented cattle, piglets, and chickens running free in sanitary barnyards.

■ As in many cultures, whiteness was long considered a mark of refinement, sophistication, and cultivation. Darker foods were considered more crude, primitive, and undesirable. In recent decades, however, health-conscious elites have reversed such associations to the extent that heavy, dark "peasant breads" are now marketed largely to the more affluent segments of the population, while white bread has more populistic appeal (Belasco 2006b: 48–50).

Since such generalizations are so broad and open to exception, it is also possible to "read" a cuisine by an intense analysis of a single favorite food. Take the Oreo, one of America's best-selling, most cherished brands. Over 360 billion of these three-layer cookies have been sold since 1912. Reading the label reveals certain prominent ingredients in the industrial diet (basic foods): refined flour, sugar, assorted vegetable oils, artificial flavors, stabilizers, preservatives, a dash of sodium, and the common denominator – maize, especially corn starch and high-fructose corn syrup (Pollan 2006: 15–119). Chocolate comes last on the label and thus constitutes the smallest ingredient – a little goes a long way. "Freshness" is asserted by the plastic wrapping as well as by the Nabisco trademark imprinted on every cookie and cracker – a symbol originating with the fifteenth-century Venetian Society of Printers and signifying "the triumph of the moral and spiritual over the evil and material." The Oreo's sculpted Maltese Cross pattern – emblem of medieval Christian warriors – further conveys a sense of loyalty, trust, honesty, and bravery. If there is a flavor principle, it is ultra-sweet, with a smear of fat (the white layer). We taste as much with our eyes as our tongues, so visual appearance is also important. The cookie's ornate carvings and fluted edges combine with the red, white, and blue packaging to convey a festive, quasi-nationalistic feeling. Stark contrasts of color (deep brown; bright white) and texture (crunchy outer layers; soft filling) also sharpen the taste appeal. An accompanying glass of milk cuts the sweetness and clears the teeth of dark crumbs. In keeping with the corporate-industrial-global nature of the American food system, the manipulative techniques that produce and preserve this pastry, and the infrastructure that supplies it, are elaborate, energy-intensive, and opaque. The cookie's cocoa and palm oil alone may travel halfway around the world.

The Oreo isn't all about business, however. As corporate, globalized, and mass-marketed as it is, the Oreo also lends itself to highly individualized consumption "protocols" – as suggested in folklorist Elizabeth Adler's food studies classic, "Creative Eating: The Oreo Syndrome" (1983). We don't all eat the same food in the same way. Rather, Oreo consumers tend to divide between those who carefully take it apart first and eat each layer separately (twisters) and those who crunch all three layers together (nibblers), as well as between those who like to "dunk" their cookie in milk and those who like it dry. While these differences may seem trivial, Adler's point is that people like to play with their food, and this is also seen in the varied approaches to eating a fried egg. "Not only do we ritualize our style of eating, we tend to separate foods that are combined. We take apart the Oreo; we eat first the white, then the yolk, of a fried egg. By attempting this separation, we create a risk, accepting a challenge to prove our control over food whose fragile quality makes it easily destructible" (5). Similar variations apply to the way we eat corn, fried potatoes, gravy and biscuits, pancakes, animal crackers (appendages first?), and entire meals. "Do you eat foods one at a time, first all the vegetables, then all the meat, then all the starches? Or do you eat a bit from each group, working your way around the plate in a circular fashion until all is gone? Do you eat your salad first, last, or with the meal? Do you drink milk or other liquids throughout the meal or gulp them down all at once at the end?" (7). Resisting the standardization and homogeneity of modern life, people like to "customize" their eating to suit personal needs and preferences. Adler suggests that those who carefully twist off all the layers and eat the sweetest one last may be categorized as "neat eaters" who like to delay gratification, while those who simply crunch the whole cookie at once are more impulsive and impatient. Pointing to some highly impressionistic demography, Nabisco's own market research claims Chicago and Philadelphia tend to be "dunking towns," while New York and Las Vegas are "twisting towns." And in an illustration of how new media technologies have enhanced customization, entire websites are devoted to discussions of how to eat Oreos and what that means. Aiming to control and "unlock the magic" of Oreo consumption, Nabisco even maintains one of the most popular fan sites. Similar forums – some corporate, some consumer-based (or "vernacular") – exist for other mass-market icons, such as Jell-O, Twinkies, Coca-Cola, and Velveeta.[1]

Personalization also applies to the way we *think* about common foods. While the Oreo may be a highly predictable "cash cow" for Nabisco and its owner, Kraft Foods, for the individual consumer it may evoke acutely poignant childhood. In "Ode to Oreos," *San Francisco Chronicle* columnist Adair Lara recalls her childhood in Marin County, California, in the 1960s: "Mother sang along to 'Steam Heat' on the record player, my sister practiced with her Hula-Hoop, and I was in love with the taste and smell and look of everything."[2] Ask a hundred people, "What do you think of when you eat an Oreo?" and you may get a hundred different answers, some intensely nostalgic, others painful, as in the student who will always associate Oreos with throwing up in the back seat during one particularly long and stressful family outing. And in a subversive appropriation of the brand name, the word "Oreo" has also been used by some African-Americans to criticize assimilationists who are "black on the outside, white on the inside." Needless to say, such usages do not appear on Nabisco's official "Oreo and Milk Memories" site.

The ability of particular foods to spark powerful personal recollections and associations leads us to another key concept of food studies: we are what we *ate*.

MADELEINES: FOOD AND MEMORY

For the connection between food and memory we inevitably turn to a very famous passage from the first volume of Marcel Proust's *Remembrance of Things Past*, Book I (1934: 34). Visiting his mother's home in the French village of Combray, Proust's stand-in protagonist Swann absent-mindedly dips a small, fluted cookie called a *madeleine* in his mother's tea. The experience is magical.

> No sooner had the warm liquid, and the crumbs with it, touched my palate than a shudder ran through my whole body, and I stopped, intent upon the extraordinary changes that were taking place. An exquisite pleasure had invaded my senses, but individual, detached, with no suggestion of its origin. And at once the vicissitudes of life had become indifferent to me, its disasters innocuous, its brevity illusory – this new sensation having had on me the effect which love has of filling me with a precious essence; or rather this essence was not in me, it was myself. I had ceased to feel mediocre, accidental, mortal. Whence could it have come to me, this all-powerful joy? I was conscious that it was connected with the taste of tea and cake, but that it infinitely transcended those savors, could not, indeed, be of the same nature as theirs. Where did it come from? What did it signify? How could I seize upon and define it? ...
>
> And suddenly the memory returned. The taste was that of the little crumb of madeleine which on Sunday mornings at Combray, ... my aunt Leonie used to give me, dipping it first in her own cup of lime-flower tea. And once I had recognized the taste of the ... madeleine soaked in her decoction of lime-flowers ..., immediately the old grey house ... rose up like the scenery of a theater to attach itself to the little pavilion, opening on to the garden, which had been built out behind it for my parents; and with the house the town ... the Square, where I was sent before luncheon, the streets along which I used to run errands, the country roads we took when it was fine. And just as the Japanese amuse themselves by filling a porcelain bowl with water and steeping in it little crumbs of paper which until then are without character or form, but, the moment they become wet, stretch themselves and bend, take on color and distinctive shape, that moment all the flowers in our garden and in M. Swann's park, and the water lilies on the Vivonne and the good folk of the village and their little dwellings and the parish church and the whole of Combray and of its surroundings, taking their proper shapes and growing solid, sprang into being, towns and gardens alike, from my cup of tea.

Proust's chance encounter proved unusually fruitful – seven volumes of fictionalized recollections. While few can be so productive, almost anyone can write a short vignette based on their personal madeleines. Some stories will be sweet, some sour, and some bittersweet. For example, I ask students to write 500 words about their own madeleines.[3] For some, powerful food memories spring immediately into mind, while others need to await some serendipitous meeting – say, a distinctive aroma encountered when entering a friend's home. Either way, the stories amply illustrate the various ways that eating reveals who we are – and are not.

For such young people these students are already profoundly nostalgic for pre-adolescent childhood. "Grandma madeleines" prevail. One writer's taste of cornbread

---

Box 2.2. Madeleines: We Are What We Ate

Food is more than an amalgam of biochemical nutrients. What we eat has enormous significance as a medium for personal recollection and collective identity. In this exercise, you are asked to reflect on a food that is especially laden with emotional, autobiographical, and symbolic meaning to you – your equivalent of the tiny cake (madeleine) that sparked French novelist Marcel Proust's seven-volume classic, *Remembrance of Things Past* (1913–1926).

Read the Proust excerpt (page 25), then think hard about your own personal madeleine. It may be anything – from a full meal to a packaged snack – as long as it's edible. Try to taste it before writing. In 500 words, describe your madeleine and the images, associations, and memories it conjures up. These images do not have to be positive, by the way. Describe, also, how you encountered this memory – for example, by chance, or by will.

You can also try classifying your madeleine:

- Is it positive, negative, or somewhere in between (bittersweet)?
- Is it a comfort food or a *dis*comfort food? A medium for conflict or reunion?
- Is it homemade or commercial?
- Is it a demographic "marker" of ethnicity, region, generation, gender, religion, or class?
- Does eating this food make you part of a group? Exclude you from other groups? (Boundary maintenance)

Note: If you can't come up with your own special madeleine, try the Oreo exercise described on pages 23–25: "When I eat an Oreo I think of ..."

For further examples of the creative use of food memories: Sutton 2001, Winegardner 1998, Reichl 1998, Boorstin 2002, Friedensohn 2006, Abu-Jaber 2005.

conjures up thoughts of her annual visits to her now departed grandparents in the rural South. "The summers spent in Alabama seem like a lifetime ago but the memories remain in my mind as if they occurred yesterday: . . . swimming at the local pool and beach, going to the movies, go-kart racing, and eating the best food that I have eaten in my life." Another African-American student recalls her grandmother's special Sunday dinners – barbecued spareribs, baked macaroni and cheese, collard greens, and, again, cornbread – consumed avidly after church and, in the fall at least, during Washington Redskins' football games. "Those were the best times of my life and all it takes is one bite of macaroni to take me back." Such recollections transcend national boundaries, as a taste of coconut chicken curry reminds one student of "my childhood in India, brought me sweet memories of my grandmother, Indian summers, power failures, good friends and the meals I looked forward to from school." Making *cafecito* [strong Cuban coffee with milk] in her dorm room returns another student to her Miami roots: "Cuban coffee provides the vehicle that allows the Cuban exile community to gather to sip the brew and discuss the anger, the mourning and painful yearning for a country in chains. It was through a simple cafecito with my dad and grandfather every Saturday and Sunday morning at the omnipresent coffee stand, hearing stories of Cuba, that help shape my identity as a Cuban."

Many stories involve similarly strong ethnic or regional "markers" – Chesapeake Bay crabs and oysters, Philadelphia cheesesteaks, boardwalk fries, baklava, kielbasa, goulash, schnitzel, chutney, pierogi, pizzelles, tamales, *puerco asado y arroz con frijoles*, *banh cuon* (Vietnamese dumplings), Korean fried fish. What makes these particularly poignant is that, when filtered through the lens of nostalgia, such memories become a way of preserving identities now perceived to be endangered by migration, mobility, and suburban mass culture.

Only a few actually welcome change, and for them the passage to adulthood may again be represented through a particular meal – as in one student's first experience (aged eighteen) with sushi, which signified both the transition to adult tastes and the high cost of such treats: "Well, the first time I ate sushi, I was ruined. It was orgasmic; even better. I knew when I took that bite of tuna that I was forever destined to a life of knowing, but not always having. (Sushi is very expensive.)" As in Eden, tasting the fruit of knowledge meant Paradise Lost. "Like the Aristotelian prisoner in the cave, I was shown a glimpse of heaven, and then led back to the world of men, where beefburgers and buffalo wings were king." A similar story relates how a college student's current binges with cheap beer pale in comparison with his first sip of alcohol – a particularly expensive brand of vodka. And another's encounter with pasta recalls an eye-opening, mouth-watering semester abroad in Rome, where fine food and a healthier, pedestrian-oriented lifestyle contrasted sharply with the car-based fast food diet of his youth; after Rome, returning to suburban America was difficult indeed.

Given that one's first conscious experience is usually at the maternal breast (or bottle), mother-related madeleines seem less likely to evoke a particular place or event than an ongoing process of parental nurturing. Just as Proust's mother offered tea and cookies to warm him up on a chilly day, mothers often prepare special foods for sick children, and these may become the "comfort foods" of adulthood – chicken soup, orange sherbet, cinnamon toast, plain rice, scrambled eggs, soft-boiled eggs cracked with a teaspoon and with white bread to dunk. Eggs seem particularly evocative this way – a reflection perhaps of their reproductive significance. Missing the small routines of childhood, some recall the foods eaten often – such as the peanut butter and jelly sandwich, or the simple *milch reis* (milk and rice) prepared by Mom and consumed every day for many years. Especially moving is the soldier's request for Mom's familiar mashed potatoes on the eve of his departure to Baghdad. Dads, too, are remembered for their recurrent feeding rituals – such as weekend pancakes, barbecues, post-game visits to McDonald's.

More bittersweet is the wistful association of the smell of cooked cabbage with a stern boarding school to which one writer and her sisters had been confined when their mother became gravely ill. And yet, she also finds that these memories "are not disturbing. What is so remarkable is the clarity of these old events, so much so that my sisters and I have been exchanging these thoughts from our past, bringing to mind old promises, feelings and bonds of sisterly love." A literary form of commensality, shared food memories overcome distance and reinforce relationships – perhaps one reason for the popularity of food memoirs.

Some are distinctly sour and establish borders, not bonds. Recently finding herself "incapacitated" by the aroma of stuffed peppers at a friend's house, one writer is transported back to a traumatic dinner of early childhood, when she balked at eating her father's special dish of rice, tomatoes, and beef – the same combination in the stuffed peppers. "Little girl," her father threatened, "if you don't eat it, you'll wear it!" and he then proceeded to dump the full plate on her head. Although she subsequently forgave her parents "for the cruel and unusual punishments they inflict on us," such incidents remind us that the family dinner table can be as much an arena for rebellion as for reunion. Along the same lines, another student's story begins with nostalgia for the aroma of Mom's cold-weather chili but then goes on to remember that, for some reason, whether digestive or cognitive, chili has always made her sick – signaling her separation, even alienation, from the rest of the family. Fixing boundaries, food reminds us of who we are *not*, as when one writer visits her spouse's Greek family and commits the "major taste-testing faux pas" of eating the bitter cloves holding his grandmother's baklava together; only an insider would know that the cloves are to be removed before biting.

Given the American antipathy to "healthy" vegetables, many negative memories involve childhood resistance to spinach, broccoli, squash, lima beans, peas, and okra. Conversely, vegetarians who reject meat at the family dinner table recall even stronger stigmatization, at least at first. Reporting on familial conflicts over meat, folklorist LuAnne K. Roth writes, "If patriotism is indeed 'the love of the good things we ate in our childhood,' as [Chinese writer, 1895–1976] Lin Yutang remarks, then it makes sense that vegetarians are initially perceived by their families to be unpatriotic, un-American, and even downright un-family like" (Roth 2005: 188). One suspects that vegetarians receive similar reactions in other carnivorous cultures as well. Noting how vegetarians can be inconvenient dinner guests, journalist Michael Pollan finds himself "inclined to agree with the French, who gaze upon any personal dietary prohibition as bad manners" (2006: 314). But historically, such "manners" are relatively recent, especially in ordinary homes, where children were generally ignored until the nineteenth century, when they became the object of more moralistic "nutritional policing" by anxious bourgeois families, by would-be reformers, and by the state itself (Coveney 2006). The intensity of family meal memories is both a product of modernity, as well as a reaction to it.

Sometimes modernity itself is the stuff of nostalgia. Akin to the way different people eat and perceive Oreos, some mass-marketed convenience foods become the subject of customized recollections: a Velveeta cheese sandwich consumed on road trips in an old VW bus to Grateful Dead concerts; an "Archway molasses cookie" purchased to reward a four-year-old for getting up early to help her now divorced father cook breakfast; a simple Handy Snack (four crackers packaged with cheese and a red stick for spreading it) routinely shared with a beloved grandfather while playing cards; or a 7-Eleven slushie bought *on the way* to grandma's. It is the cheap, artificially flavored crushed ice, not grandma's home cooking, that sparks this memory. For one writer, the unorthodox blend of Lay's potato chips and plain cottage cheese recalls visits to grandma, who claims to have invented this family snack. (According to market researchers Brian Wansink and Cynthia Sangerman, 2000, potato chips are America's favorite comfort food.) For a former Little Leaguer, Gatorade evokes "old teammates, hot summer days, triple headers, harsh defeats, and brilliant victories." In an R-rated version, the "pop" of Gatorade's "freshness seal" suggests trips with high school friends to the beach, where – in a taste of the complex sexual rituals of teenage boys – they drank massive amounts of Citrus Cooler as a purported cure for "blue balls" (a euphemism for painfully unconsummated male sexual arousal). And, belying the conventional wisdom that mass culture endangers family life, students warmly recall the mass-produced foods eaten with family members while watching television together. Eating normally proscribed "junk foods" on sick days while watching daytime TV is another common memory.

Given the mind-bending power of madeleines, it is inevitable that some have attempted to channel those memories toward social goals more significant than merely fulfilling a professor's assignment or selling a memoir. In *Remembrance of Repasts: An Anthropology of Food and Memory* (2001), David Sutton shows how Greek islanders plan elaborate feasts with the conscious goal of having them remembered collectively later on; conversely their keen ability to remember and discuss particular meals many years later prolongs the community-building function (commensality) of social eating. In perhaps the grimmest example of how food memories can empower people, starving concentration camp inmates during the Second World War found emotional sustenance by sharing recipes for meals past. *In Memory's Kitchen: A Legacy from the Women of Terezin* (1996), editor Cara De Silva sees such memories as a form of resistance "to those who want to annihilate you and your cultures and traditions, and everything about you ... By writing [them down, the women] were using these as weapons. They were using potato doughnuts and dumplings, and stuffed eggs, and caramels from Bonn, instead of bombs and bazookas" (quoted in Rosofsky 2004: 52). In a variation, affluent descendants of slaves, famine survivors, war refugees, and impoverished immigrants will cherish the stigmatized foods of their oppressive past as a way to honor their ancestors' courage and endurance – for example, the simple but fragrant biscuits of a mill town tenement, the scrounged "hedge nutrition" of Ireland, the "Geechie Rice" of the Sea Islands, the unleavened bread of the Jewish Exodus, the boiled chicken feet of Chinese peasants (Avakian 1997). And remembering even the most distasteful foods of the past may have some survival value. Lacking many of the genetically programmed "instincts" of the more selective species, omnivores may employ memories as a way to distinguish the harmful from the wholesome. The longer the memory, the longer the life (Pollan 2006: 287–298).

Madeleines can also be exploited for commercial purposes. Whether in Disney-world or Bali, the vacation industry is well known for its stereotypical representation of so-called "traditional foods," which have become an essential ingredient in "culinary tourism" (Long 2003, Halter 2000, Heldke 2003). Anthropologist Richard Wilk shows that a distinctively "Belizean" cuisine emerged not so much from the ordinary citizens of Belize – an exceptionally multicultural society – as from the pressure of nostalgic expatriates and authenticity-seeking travelers (2002, 2006). A somewhat similar dynamic is seen in anthropologist Carla Guerron-Montero's study of the Bocas del Toro region of Panama, where locals learned to serve the Spanish-style meals that tourists expected, rather than the very different Afro-Antillean cuisine of the area (2004). Attempting to cash in on "heritage tourism," the declining industrial city of Pueblo, Colorado built a new identity around the once despised chili pepper (Haverluk 2002). In a classic study of such "neo-localism," historian Kolleen Guy suggests that the legendary French *terroir* that one supposedly detects in a taste of good Bordeaux or brie was in fact the relatively recent concoction of an opportunistic alliance among nationalist politicians, ambitious growers, and tourist chateau operators all seeking to serve their narrow economic interests while stifling the competition from seemingly less "authentic" locales (2002). An analogous process took place in Victorian America, when descendants of the original British colonists consciously invented the components of the now familiar Thanksgiving dinner – roast turkey, stuffing, pumpkin pie – as a way to assert their superiority to newcomers who arrived with radically different cultures and cuisines (Smith 2004).

Similarly, advertisements for McDonald's, Frosted Flakes, Kraft Macaroni and Cheese, and Kool-Aid may take advantage of childhood associations with processed foods to build loyalty for their brands (and for industrial food in general). Such associations "work" best if they tap dominant myths. According to its advertising, a bite of sausage at Bob Evans's Farm Restaurant "takes me back home" – but only if my home resembles a Currier and Ives print of a prosperous Ohio farmstead. And, as we have seen, Nabisco even has a website where consumers of Oreos – the national madeleine? – can exchange their memories, but only the positive ones. One does wonder about whether such mass-mediated recollections will further homogenize the modern mind, producing "McMemories." Yet just as the playing of a "golden oldie" song may spark vastly different recollections of teenage life, so too may consumers experience and recall a Big Mac and fries in very specialized ways. A similar "localization" occurs in the way specific cultures view and reinterpret globalized fast foods: a Big Mac in Beijing may "mean" something quite different from a Big Mac in Chicago (Watson 1997). Similarly, Tim Horton donuts are prized as an ironic emblem of Canadian national identity precisely because they seem "simple," "humble," and thus un-American, even though they are now mass-produced by Wendy's, an American corporation (Penfold 2002).

Along with imparting meaning to our daily lives, these rich linkages between food and identity pose major challenges to those who worry about responsibility – the costs and consequences of what we eat. If pot roast, bacon-laden collards, or chicken curry recall Grandma, it becomes hard to see much evil in the animal industry. If a Happy Meal or pizza reminds us of dinner with Dad after the soccer match, then rejecting fat means rejecting Dad. The same might be said of a post-hockey game Tim Horton donut, sugar and trans fats notwithstanding. Can we really label Grandma and Dad "irresponsible" and "deadbeats"? If Nabisco is beloved for its Oreos, can we really be angry at its former corporate parent, Philip Morris? By renaming its food divisions Altria (with the same word root as "altruism"), Philip Morris certainly hoped to obscure its identity as a tobacco marketer.[4]

Further difficulties result from the uncertain nature of identity in a mobile, multi-cultural world. If "we are what we eat," who are "we" anyway? How many people does it take to comprise a "we"? And in what context? As voters? As soldiers? Cooks? Customers? Do we define a group's identity by bioregion, by foodshed, by arbitrary lines drawn on an inaccurate map two hundred years ago by imperial politicians, by the selective recollections of aging immigrants? An especially vivid example of the last difficulty can be seen in Barry Levinson's film, *Avalon* (1990), which traces the progress of a large Baltimore Jewish family through three generations. In an early scene, the extended immigrant family crowds a small row house for a Thanksgiving feast. While the family has no interest in the holiday's Anglo-American history, they do value this annual ritual as an opportunity to remember the old country and their early struggles in America. Yet the fallibility of memory is accentuated in a disagreement over whether one crucial event – the arrival of the family's patriarch – took place in midsummer or midwinter. As if to emphasize the subjectivity of remembrances, Levinson reenacts The Father's arrival twice, in both seasons. More-over, to demonstrate the elusiveness of memory in a culture that values youth above age, the Thanksgiving gatherings become increasingly contentious over the years, as the children grow impatient with their elders' stories. Near the end a much smaller nuclear family – a mere sliver of the original clan – is seen eating its dinner in silence, in front of the TV. Perhaps to be an American is to forget, *not* remember. To be sure, memory, like taste, may fade with age everywhere. In Ang Lee's *Eat Drink Man Woman* (1994), a retired Taiwanese chef attempts to keep his splintering family together by cooking elaborate Sunday banquets, only to discover that he has lost his ability to taste. Rather than binding his daughters with pleasant tastes of the past, his nearly inedible dishes almost drive them away.

And what about the phrase "what we eat"? We eat so many different foods! Which ones signify deep identity and which simply fill us up? Culinarians like to draw deep distinctions between human "dining," which is full of deep cultural significance, and animal "feeding," a purely biological act, but not everything we eat has a lot of meaning. Sometimes we just "feed." And then there is that troublesome identity verb "are," derived from "to be." What is identity anyway? Can we even be sure of our own personality or "character," much less the defining qualities of broader entities such as "neighborhood," "region," or "nation"? What about those of us who come from several different ethnic or racial backgrounds? In an affecting study of Korean-American adoptees, social worker Kathleen Ja Sook Berquist finds people caught between markers – not really Asian, not fully American either. When well-meaning white parents attempt to cultivate their children's Korean identity with iconic foods such as kim chee, moon cakes, and bulgolgi, the adoptees may come away feeling even more alienated. "Food as an access point creates an awareness of the estranged position adoptees find themselves in and the incompleteness of their cultural memory. Instead of feeding a hunger [for identity], it exposes a void" (2006: 150). Sometimes people may feel most "whole," most like "themselves," over neutral food. For example, in Spike Lee's *Jungle Fever* (1991), a mixed race New York couple escapes from equally intolerant Bensonhurst (Italian) and Harlem (African-American) by sharing takeout Chinese food in blandly corporate midtown Manhattan. Similarly, sociologists Gaye Tuchman and Harry Gene Levine argue that second generation Jewish New Yorkers took to Chinese food because it seemed so "cosmopolitan, urbane, and sophisticated" – i.e., less confining or "provincial" than the kosher Eastern European fare of their parents (1993: 164). And anthropologist James Watson writes that the Chinese youth of Hong Kong embraced McDonald's, "precisely because it was *not* Chinese"; that is it seemed more "laid-back" and "non-hierarchical" (Watson 1997: 86). In all, we don't always want to eat "what we are."

What if Walt Whitman's "Song of Myself" was right in claiming that the self is so full of contradictions and uncertainties as to be "not a bit tamed" and ultimately "untranslatable"?[5] It doesn't take psychoanalysis or romantic poetry to tell us that if our personal identities are so elusive, our collective affiliations must be much more so. And the confusion does not apply to just modern or postmodern cuisines. Richard Wilk has shown that ever since the first pirates arrived in the sixteenth century, Belizean food practices have been "heterogeneous, polyglot, disorderly, and even incoherent" – an apt description, perhaps, of human cuisines in general (2002: 79).

So, returning to our original culinary triangle, we may find that deciding what to eat may be complicated not only by considerations of convenience and responsibility, but also by conflicts within identity itself.

Chapter Summary

- Dining is more than feeding.
- All cultures have a "cuisine," which consists of a distinctive set of basic foods, flavor principles, preparation techniques, rules for consumption, and a supply infrastructure for getting food from field to fork.
- Foods have different symbolic "weights." Some are "tortillas" — simple, daily staples — while others are "tamales" — time-consuming dishes reserved for special occasions (Williams 1984).
- According to the concept of *commensality*, sharing food has almost magical properties in its ability to turn self-seeking individuals into a collaborative group.
- Many of the dining practices that we take to be timeless and universal are in fact highly variable and only recently "constructed."
- Resisting the standardization and homogeneity of modern life, people like to "customize" their eating to suit personal needs and preferences.
- We are what we ate.
- Food memories can serve many personal, social, political, and economic purposes.
- We don't always want to eat "what we are."

3 THE DRAMA OF FOOD: DIVIDED IDENTITIES

Do I contradict myself? Very well, then I contradict myself, I am large, I contain multitudes.

Walt Whitman (1819–1892)

The test of a first-rate intelligence is the ability to hold two opposed ideas in mind at the same time and still retain the ability to function.

F. Scott Fitzgerald (1896–1940)

The greatest conflicts are not between two people but between one person and himself.

Garth Brooks (b. 1962)

If conflict is the soul of drama, then food studies makes for very good theater. It is no surprise that playwrights, storytellers, filmmakers, songwriters, and visual artists often use food to hold our attention (i.e., to entertain us) with interesting tensions and contradictions. In this chapter, we draw on these expressive forms, along with more conventional social and historical data, to illustrate some of the most compelling conflicts within our sense of "who we are." Conflicts among identity, convenience, and responsibility – the larger triangle – will follow in later chapters.

FOOD AND SEXUALITY

The connections between food and sex are primal. Both are central to biological reproduction and to the establishment of strong social ties. Both involve the incorporation of outside entities within the private body. Both are highly personal, indeed intimate; both involve the primary senses of sight, smell, touch, and, yes, taste. In *Carnal Appetites: FoodSexIdentities*, gender studies scholar Elspeth Probyn argues that "Practices of preparing and eating food are … highly sensual and sometimes sexual … The simple point is that the hands-on encounter with food connects us with surfaces, textures, tastes, smells, insides, and outsides" (2000: 60). Both food and sex require sustained use of the mouth. Anthropologists Peter Farb and George Armelagos report that "When the Aborigines of Central Australia ask the question, '*Utna ilkukabaka?*' it may mean either 'Have you eaten' or 'Have you had sexual intercourse?'" (1980: 85; Allen 2000: 29). Sex creates children, who are bound to their mothers through food; mothers in turn use sex and food to bind fathers to their family. The body parts that are vital for reproduction are richly endowed with complex, often contradictory culinary meanings of love and hate, attraction and disgust (Allen 2000).

Farb and Armelagos summarize these linkages: "According to the Judeo-Christian tradition, eating the fruit of knowledge in the Garden of Eden was followed by sexual shame; first came food, then sex … The close connection between eating and sex is not hard to explain if it is assumed that early in the evolution of the human species males and females were brought together primarily by the two basic necessities for survival – food and procreation" (1980: 136). Hence the suggestively ambiguous title of their book, *Consuming Passions* – a title also employed by at least one other food studies text (Griffiths and Wallace 1998), as well as by one "delightfully quirky memoir of an adventurous food-obsessed life" (West 2000), a sober critique of popular culture (Williamson 1985), a history of the courtesans of classical Athens (Davidson 1999), an archeological study of cannibalism (Cole 2006), a cultural history of Victorian "leisure and pleasure" (Flanders 2006), a gourmet's history of British taste (Pullar 1970), a British university course on consumer culture, an Australian television cooking program, a website for a wedding cake bakery, a 1989 film "about a chocolate factory that begins putting out boxes of chocolates made out of human flesh,"[1] and a performance artist's video exploring "the passion for sweets as a replacement for a sense of security and a source of erotic satisfaction."[2] When reading culinary literature it is often hard to discern a clear line between kitchen and bedroom – as in cookbook writer Elizabeth David's eroticized description of cassoulet in *Mediterranean Food* (1950): "creamy," "tender," "juicy," "moist," "smoking hot." The overlap was intentional, literary critic Alice McLean writes, as "The pleasures of eating and, to a certain extent, sex were a definitive source of inspiration for David, who broke with the conventional female pattern of behavior in both her written work and her personal life" (McLean: 2004, 41, 43).

The shared ambiguities of food and sex make food metaphors very attractive to storytellers attempting to express the complexities of love (and, conversely, to describe the sensual pleasures of eating). Take, for example, the vast library of popular love/ hate songs that employ food imagery. If there's a "flavor principle" in love lyrics,

Box 3.1. "Consuming Passions" in Popular Culture

Select a song, story, film, or television program that has a lot of food content. Analyze this "text" for the contradictory aspects of cooking and dining, including:

- As a tool of commensality (bringing people together) and exclusion (separating Us from Other), conviviality and conflict (the battle of the dinner table).
- As an enabler of or substitution for sexual relationships.
- As a means by which people communicate (voice).
- As a demographic marker (gender, race, class, region, etc.).
- As a means of empowerment for the cook.
- As an expression of resistance or rebellion.
- As tragedy (e.g., gangster kills an enemy in a restaurant) and comedy, especially irony (e.g., gangsters discuss their sauce recipes).
- As sexual metaphor, including "basic foods" (especially meat and seafood), "manipulative techniques" (spooning, churning, grilling) and "flavor principles" (sweet, sour, spicy, salty, bitter, hot).
- As a narrative device, especially the way meals are used to advance the plot, enable key conversations, and ground characters in daily rituals.

For supplementary reading: Bower 2004, Inness 2001a, Parasecoli 2004, Baron 2006, Tompkins 2005, Fitzpatrick 2007, Morton 2004.

it tends to be sweet: romantic ballads abound with images of sugar, honey, jam, candy, cookies, peaches, cupcakes, babycakes, pies, nectar, and in tropical countries, mangoes. As love warms into lust, however, flavors shift toward salt – the taste of human secretions – and the "hotter" spices, especially pepper, ginger, garlic, and mustard. And if candies and pastries are the "basic foods" of innocent romance, meat and seafood are the staples of sex. Joined with other eroticized high-calorie dishes – buns, biscuits, dumplings, shortnin' bread, whipped cream, butter, cheesecake, tarts, tamales, jelly rolls, custards, gravy, sauce, mayonnaise – the foods of love certainly raise the heat. And we may even be biologically programmed that way, for successful reproduction requires calories; as economist Thomas Malthus contended in 1798, the more calories available to a population, the higher the birth rate. Conversely, dis-taste is expressed as sour, cold, bitter, hard. No one wants a "tough cookie," a "hard-boiled" sourpuss, or overaged "mutton" – Elizabethan slang for a prostitute, the antithesis of the cute lamb chop, or virginal "fresh meat." Elisabeth Rozin's "manipulative techniques" also figure in the gastro-pornographic vocabulary, as phrases such as "spooning," "creaming," "beating," "mashing," "churning," "grilling," "grinding," "frying," and "home cooking" all have double meanings – as do tools such as "oven" and, the anti-sex opposite, "deep freeze" (Allen 2000).

As with madeleines, these intensely sexualized associations between eating and loving make it difficult to adopt the asceticism implied in eating responsibly. If pastry, sugar, fat, meat, and salt are so closely tied to life's most intimately pleasurable experiences, who would ever want to cut back on them?

To be sure, as eating has become more problematic in recent decades – perhaps due to the mounting worries about poisons, fatness, environmental degradation, worker exploitation, and so on (see Chapters 5 and 6) – the number of foods and spices considered to be aphrodisiacs has decreased markedly, as has the food-based vocabulary of love. This downscaling may also reflect the fact that in modern times, food is cheaper, more abundant, and thus more taken for granted than ever. For comparison, consider the extensive menus of popular songs of the early and middle twentieth century – a period when most people were more worried about avoiding hunger than about eating too much. For example Fats Waller's "You're My Dish" (1937) likens the 300lb jazz pianist's love interest to peaches and cream, angel cake, Yorkshire pudding, French pastries, and "a tantalizing, appetizing blue plate of romance."[3] Like Waller, blues queen Bessie Smith was a large person who indulged all senses, and that full-charge sensuality came through clearly (and pornographically) in "Kitchen Man" (co-penned by Eubie Blake and Waller's partner Andy Razaf), where, following a classic upstairs/downstairs affair, the "quite deluxe" "Madam Bucks" laments the sudden departure of plain Dan, "her kitchen man." Proving that humans are true omnivores, virtually every food becomes an object of lust, even cabbage, hash, succotash, and turnip tops. Only after exhausting the vegetable kingdom does Madam Bucks finally and ravenously move toward the basic foods of love: meat (chops, frankfurters, hams), seafood (clams), and pastry (donuts). Similarly, Fats Waller's "You're not the only oyster in the stew" (1934) assumed an abundance of tastes, both culinary and sexual, even to the point where romantic meaning could be suggested in the follow-up line, "You're not the only wrinkle in the prune."

We can find a comparable relish for a wide variety of foods in traditional country songs such as Hank Williams's 1951 "Jambalaya," a salute to the spicy feast of "Cajun paella," crawfish pie, and file gumbo, served lovingly by his "cher amio" at a bayou feast. Likewise, in "Hey Good Lookin'" (1951), Williams expresses an openness to "cookin' up" some new "recipes," whether culinary or romantic. And when cornetist Louis Armstrong went "Struttin' with some barbecue" (1927) he may well

have been referring to a pimp parading down the street with "partic[...]
young women" (Allen 2000: 35) – a meaning of "Barbie" perhaps unk[...]
doll-makers at Mattell.

For a more modest – and now archaic – declaration of domestic affection, lowly organ meats serve well in "Kidney Stew" (1947), in which saxophonist Eddie "Cleanhead" Vinson resolves to go back home to his "old gal Sue," who "ain't caviar / Just plain old kidney stew." For bluesman Champion Jack Dupree, it's "She cooks me cabbage" (1955) – a fondness also seen in the French term of endearment, "Mon petit chou chou," as well as in Bessie Smith's craving for "turnip tops." The association between domestic comfort and down-home foods is reflected in the slang term, "chitlin chasin'" – defined by UrbanDictionary.com as "A guy who pretends to be the committed boyfriend to a girl solely because he knows she loves to cook great home-style meals for her man every night." But one feels considerably more heat in Junior Wells's instrumental track, "Chitlins con Carne," as well as in the JBs' funky "Pass the Peas," and in Booker T and the MGs' "Green Onions" – all of which evoke the raucous Jim Crow clubs where the food, like the music, was spicy, high octane, and cooked from scratch. Such associations continue in Afro-Caribbean "salsa" (sauce) – as in the neo-traditional songs of Jose Conde y Ola Fresca, whose 2006 album *Ay que Rico!* includes a "menu" of suggestive songs such as "Puerco Robao" (stolen pork?) and "Bolitas de Arroz con Pollo" (chicken and yellow rice balls), whose lyrics are worthy of Waller and Smith: "Two little balls and a plantain … on your plate, I will serve it hot and tasty for you."[4] Conversely, older songs describing love's denial or limits assumed that listeners would also understand an impoverished life where food itself appeared in tiny doses, as in Mississippi-born Willie Dixon's "Spoonful" (1953), where men fight, lie, and die for "one little spoon of your precious love." In Dixon's economy of scarcity, Malthusian conditions may govern the distribution of food and love alike, so the bountiful periods are appreciated more.

Similarly, when singing of love's inevitable woes and shortcomings, the more traditional songs embrace a diverse menu of metaphoric foods. In Fats Waller's elusive ballad of domestic discontent, "Too Much Meat and No Potatoes" (1941), a marital diet of straight meat (sex?) without the starchy "sides" makes for an imbalanced, unripened relationship, "like green tomatoes." Waller's frustrated protagonist would even settle for some peas, for "with meat 'most anything goes" – a line that aptly summarizes a genuinely omnivorous approach to food and sex. Likewise, The Swallows' 1951 rhythm and blues classic, "It Ain't the Meat, It's the Motion," suggests that there's more to a relationship than plain body parts. The pleasure of social eating – commensality – depends on context: it's not the dinner, it's the diners who make a meal tasty and memorable. This principle was stated quite succinctly in Proverbs 15:17: "Better is a dinner of herbs where love is, than a fatted ox in the midst of hatred" (Egerton 1994: 171). And also in a Slovakian proverb: "Better to eat bread in peace, than cake amidst turmoil" (Egerton 1994: 71).

Closer to their roots in food production, earlier urban blues audiences could also easily understand the agricultural references in Washboard Sam's charge of infidelity (1939): "Somebody's been digging my potatoes." Firsthand knowledge of the food chain is also implied in Muddy Waters' "Long Distance Call" (1951), in which a "loser" (cuckold) is cruelly informed that there is "another mule kickin' in your stall."

Drawing on the same country blues traditions, Sleepy John Estes's "Milk Cow Blues" (1930) (most famously covered by teenaged Elvis Presley) suggested dairy analogies that perhaps only someone with rural roots could appreciate, especially an abandoned spouse's longing for the "butter" of his wayward "milk cow." Anthropologist Carole Counihan reports a similar gender ideology in the traditional Tuscan saying that men should choose "women and cattle from your own villages" (*moglie e buoi dai paesi tuoi*) (2004: 115). Taking this bovine analogy to an extreme, Nigerian Arab women are deliberately fattened up like their husbands' hefty cattle. Both are seen as "potent symbols of their menfolk's success" (Popenoe 2005: 18); conversely, overly thin Western women are likened to "scrawny cows" (13).

In more recent years, however, with the growing distance between field and plate, such agricultural references disappear from popular lyrics, as do the more complex, diversified, labor-intensive meals. (To be a "cow" nowadays, according to UrbanDictionary.com, is to be fat, promiscuous, and offensive – certainly never attractive.⁵) In "Burger Man" (1990) by Texas rock/blues band ZZ Top, there are no blue-plate specials or cherry pies or fresh milk, just red, greasy beef, grilled fast, hot, and plain. Satirizing the more upfront sexuality of recent decades, fellow Texan Kinky Friedman urges, "Get your biscuits in the oven, and your buns in bed" (1973). Compare Hank Williams's sentimental ode to jambalaya with the stark description of how to eat crawfish offered by The Radiators, a New Orleans rock band (1987): "Suck the head, squeeze the tip." It's hard to tell whether Annihilator's "Kraft Dinner" (1990) is about a human relationship, but clearly this thrash metal band has a rather attenuated relationship with cooking. Instead, food, perhaps like love, must be delivered fast, "now."

Likewise, the family meal served in The Who's "Heinz Baked Beans" (1967) does not seem likely to stimulate warm or lengthy "remembrances" of domestic bliss. Recent songs of discord are similarly prosaic, as in bluesman Albert Collins's complaint (1966) about "Too many dirty dishes."

Of course, a broader menu of risqué double entendres can still be found on the Internet, where sites such as Foodporn.com promise to fill "all your delicious dreams, delightful desires, and forbidden fantasies" with pages suggestively titled "barely legal," "self-pleasuring," "hardcore," and "table dance." Yet clicking on these links yields excellent recipes for food, but little insight into human sexuality – other than vague suggestions that, rather than supplementing sex, food now *substitutes* for it.

It is unclear why food and sex have become so disconnected. Perhaps the availability of more brazenly pornographic imagery in mass media has reduced the need for the sly innuendos of Fats Waller and Bessie Smith. And it may also be that, in the age of AIDS and mad cow disease, both sexuality and food are seen as far more troublesome today. Elspeth Probyn takes this one step further and suggests that tasteless fast food has so desensualized and desexualized us that "Sexuality currently risks becoming theoretically stale, past its use-by date" (2000: 60). An optimist might also consider this more hopeful spin: perhaps the apparent relegation of X-rated food metaphors to the more "hard core" zones of popular music reflects a growing reluctance to objectify the opposite sex, just as the cruder forms of racism and sexism – once ubiquitous in mainstream discourse – have diminished considerably in "respectable" society. Whereas it was quite acceptable for a politician of the 1930s to refer to blacks as "niggers" and women as "dishes" or "tomatoes," nowadays either reference might produce an immediate uproar.

FOOD AND GENDER

But then again, maybe not. Just as gender relations and sexuality remain problematic, there is no doubt that food presents conflicted identities for women. Is food a tool of female empowerment or enslavement? Agency or objectification? Pleasure or anguish?

On the one hand, preparing and serving food has long given women power. In hunting and gathering societies, women find most of the calories – perhaps as much as 85 percent among New England natives of the colonial period (Merchant 1989: 82). Women have always played a primary role in agriculture, too, and in much of the Third World they remain the primary food providers for the household. According to the UN's Food and Agriculture Organization (FAO), "Women produce more than 50 percent of the food grown worldwide. This includes up to 80 percent of food produced by women in African countries, 60 percent in Asia and between 30 and 40 percent in South America."[6] Of western Kenyan women, anthropologist Michael Dietler writes, "Women are the agricultural and culinary labor force that lies behind the production of all Luo feasts ... Women grow the crops, process them, and do the cooking." Hence the need for several wives as a prerequisite for mounting the large feasts that signal a family's prestige (2001: 99). Women have also sold food for income, ranging from "butter and egg money" to full-scale boarding

---

Box 3.2. Women, Food, and Conflict

Interview an older woman who cooks a lot about her personal relationship with food and cooking. To what extent is food a means of empowerment and to what extent is it a means of oppression? What is the economic value of her "foodwork"? How does she manage the more onerous aspects of foodwork? Does she use convenience foods? If so, does she attempt to personalize them? How does she attempt to cater (or not) to the tastes of family members? How does she use food to "tame" men? Is she "cooked out," or does she still like to cook? Record her food voice, the way she uses food to communicate her identity and bind others to herself. How much "kitchen talk" goes on in her household? How and where does she shop for food? Ask, also, for a brief history of how her kitchen chores and expectations have changed over the years. Has she become more health-conscious? To what extent does she rely on mass media for new recipes? And look at her cookbooks and recipe collections for personal favorites and comments. How might her recipes be read as a form of memoir or autobiography? (Jansen 1997, Theophano 2002, Steinberg 2007). Finally, to what extent do her food experiences reflect the conflicts discussed in this chapter?

For supplementary reading: Murcott 1983, Avakian 1997, Avakian and Haber 2005, Shapiro 2004, DeVault 1991, Inness 2001b, Abarca 2001, Counihan 2004.

---

houses, restaurants, and catering services. In *Building Houses Out of Chicken Legs: Black Women, Food, and Power* (2006), historian Psyche Williams-Forson shows how African-American women have supported families, paid mortgages, and educated their children through the sale of fried chicken.

Even when women are restricted to feeding just their own immediate family, they find leverage through cooking. For one thing, control of the kitchen often translates into control of domestic consumption; as "gatekeepers," cooks manage a household's imports of nutrients and its exports of money. Obviously women have enormous power over children, and through their foodwork they may hold families together. Sociologist Marjorie DeVault writes that "Women often choose to provide service because they recognize that their work contributes to sociability in groups, and sometimes to a group's very survival" (1991: 233). A Tuscan father told anthropologist Carole Counihan, "Eating together is the foundation of the family" (2004: 117). Even the cynical Oscar Wilde recognized the healing function of good home cooking: "After a good dinner, one can forgive anybody, even one's own relations" (Egerton 1994: 124).

Through food women may also tame men. Such control has survival value for women, as good cooking *may* be a defense against domestic violence – a tactic suggested by temperance crusaders who argued that the best way to keep husbands out of saloons was good home cooking. "Do not grumble about the saloon until you have put some soup in its place," home economics pioneer Ellen Richards argued in 1896 (Levenstein 1988: 49). Conversely, a husband's failures could be attributed to his wife's indifferent housekeeping, as seen in an 1868 domestic advice manual: "Many a day-laborer, on his return at evening from his hard toil is repelled by the sight of a disorderly house and a comfortless supper ... and he makes his escape to the grog-shop or the underground gambling room" (Green and Perry 2003: 59). Of course, there is a considerable displacement of responsibility in this formulation, for women are thus blamed for failures in a realm they do not control – the male sphere.

Anthropologist Brett Williams shows that Tejano (Hispanic Texan) migrant women collaborate in the extremely labor-intensive process of tamale-making in order "to knit families together, to obligate both male and female kin, and to nurture and bind their husbands as well." Such influential relationships help to sustain the "convoys of kin" that travel together to harvest the crops. And since tamales vary greatly by region, their preparation on the road reminds migrant workers of their roots and thereby neutralizes some of the inherent instability of road life (Williams 1984: 115). In *The Migrant's Table*, sociologist Krishnendu Ray shows how, in another form of resistance to the disruptions of mobility, middle-class Bengali-American immigrant women consciously embrace the "asymmetrical," time-consuming labor of preparing rice and *jhol* (fish) dinners, as a way of warding off the perceived "collapse" of neighboring "Western" families" (2004: 126). Similarly, Counihan's Tuscan subjects consciously use memories of traditional foods to mobilize opposition to the culinary degradation supposedly wrought by modernization (2004: 27). Reading Italian activist Carlo Petrini's neo-traditional manifesto, *Slow Food: The Case for Taste* (2001), one may be struck by his clear nostalgia for the pre-modern "family conviviality" of the time *before* women entered the workforce en masse (66–67). For "post-feminists" who blame the decline of civilization on the purported decline of family dinner, the power women gained through outside employment was not enough to compensate for the power lost to convenience food marketers McDonald's, Philip Morris, and Nestlé.

But even if many women no longer cook "from scratch," they still do most of the shopping, food preparation, and cleaning up – even in the most convenience-oriented society, the US.[7] It is puzzling that so many husbands remain dependent on wives for sustenance, for why *would* anyone cede so much hegemony over basic biological needs to someone else? "If you like good food," wrote Chinese author and actor Li Liweng (1611–1676), "cook it yourself" (Egerton 1994: 172). The Beatles' simple question asking whether they will still be fed when they are sixty-four years old is no idle inquiry, for according to the "widower effect," male health may decline rapidly after a nurturing wife dies. Perhaps many women retain this caretaking role because they *like* the control it gives them.

One way of conceptualizing this power is through community nutritionist Annie Hauck-Lawson's idea of "food voice": in societies that do not want to listen to women, food gives them a "say." Recipes, kitchen talk (*charlas cocinas*), memoirs, and community cookbooks all offer satisfying ways to communicate their experiences, preferences, observations, and desires (Hauck-Lawson 1992, Abarca 2001, Finn 2004). Reading through her mother's collection of stained, annotated recipes, one literature professor realized that her otherwise quiet, self-effacing mother was actually "an accomplished writer" whose scrawled commentaries addressed complex issues of taste, economics, authority, and competence (Jansen 1997: 55). For folklorist Janet Theophano, old cookbooks offer a rich insight into the lives of "barely articulate" forgotten women. "Long overlooked ... these intimate stories reveal individual women telling their own life stories, their versions of their communities, and the visions they have of society and culture" (2002: 3). Similarly, in her study of women's letters to the editor, food columns, and other advice exchanges, Laura Shapiro (2004) finds a complex and sophisticated discussion of the emotional, economic, and political pressures on homemakers of the 1950s. In fact, if food gives "voice" to the disempowered, some women sing gloriously through their dishes. And sometimes they do so in choirs – as in the community cookbooks compiled by groups of women for charitable, religious, and civic causes (Bower 1997).

At the same time, food can obviously confine women to subservient roles, keeping them busy at home and "quiet" in the public sphere. In this view, food controls women – to the extent that, just as temperance reformers warned, women who do not fulfill their husband's culinary (and sexual) expectations may find themselves subject to abandonment and violence (Murcott 1983). The bedroom-kitchen orbit of domestic confinement is expressed quite brutally in "Shake, Rattle and Roll" (1954), in which Big Joe Turner orders his wife/girlfriend "outta that bed" and "in that kitchen," where she is to make some "noise with the pots and pans."

One can rightly wonder how much leverage such servitude actually offered. Dietler observes that even though Kuo women of Kenya provide all the food for their husbands' feasts, the credit goes to the men; and where women do stage their own feasts for other women, these tend to be on a smaller scale (2001: 92). Catering to children's whimsies is also strenuous and perilous – as in the case of the *obentos* (boxed lunches) carefully prepared by Japanese mothers for picky children who must eat every bite quickly lest mother and pupil be chastised by school authorities (Allison 1997: 298). Moreover, why is it assumed that mothers must be the primary caterers? Even mothers' seemingly timeless and universal role as the main domesticated feeders of infants can be contested. After all, while breast milk *may* be preferable for newborns (experts disagree), it can be pumped for bottle delivery by men; infants can also be breastfed by paid wet nurses, and, if mothers do want to nurse, there is no inherently "natural" reason why breastfeeding needs to be sequestered from the public sphere. Much of what is assumed to be archetypal may be viewed as a social construction of patriarchy. In the case of the Japanese *obentos*, anthropologist Anne Allison sees "mothering as gendered ideological state apparatus" (305). And illustrating our theme of divided identity, Allison sees *obento*-making as "a double-edged sword for women": both creative self-expression and a reflection of her subordination to ritual and authority (307).

Whether female or male, foodwork is strenuous, hot, tedious, repetitive, and often unappreciated. Of Mexico, historian Jeffrey Pilcher writes, "'Hard but sure,' traditional Mesoamerica cooking required enormous effort"; preparing the staple tortillas alone could require five to six hours a day (Pilcher 1998: 10, 102). No wonder then that most modern Mexican women buy them pre-made. Similarly, in her compelling "Plea for Culinary Modernism," historian Rachel Laudan argues that twentieth-century Japanese women "welcomed factory-made bread because they could sleep in a little longer instead of having to get up to make rice ... Working women in India are happy to serve commercially made bread during the week, saving the time-consuming business of making chapattis for the weekend. As supermarkets appeared in Eastern Europe and Russia, housewives rejoiced at the choice and convenience of ready-made goods" (2001: 42).

If prepared convenience foods have replaced home cooking, *in*convenience did not necessarily foster it. That is, the ability to express oneself, to assert power and voice as a home cook, is partly determined by the equipment at hand. For most of history (and for much of the world today) cooking facilities were spare and ill-equipped. Before the modern era, few homes had decent stoves, ovens, or even separate "kitchens," and energy was scarce (Mennell 1996: 49). One reason why the potato was so eagerly embraced throughout the world was that it could be roasted quickly over an open fire and eaten with bare hands, as plates and utensils were scarce, too (Diner 2001: 92). Similarly, stir-frying and sautéing conserved energy, time, and nutrients in stressed peasant societies. And what was alcohol but a quick and easy way to store and consume calories? (Pollan 2006: 100–102). Even in the late nineteenth century, home cooking was not an option for many urban working-class American women, historian Katherine Leonard Turner argues. "Among other considerations, fuel for cooking was expensive, good stoves were rare and a worker's time could be better spent earning wages than producing cooked food at home." Despite much nostalgic moralizing about the good old days, *these* pragmatic Victorians purchased processed convenience foods from groceries and pre-cooked takeout foods from bakeries, saloons, lunchrooms, delis, and pushcarts. Rejecting the efforts of middle-class reformers to encourage home cooking, "The working-class women of Boston simply weren't interested in 'slow foods' … They were already accustomed to picking up bread and cake for their daily meals. The 'pie stands and bakeshops' may not have been nutritious or particularly frugal, but they were an important neighborhood source of quick, cheap food" (2006: 14–15). Likewise, fast food was popular in European cities long before the founding of White Castle (1921), Howard Johnson's (1925), or McDonald's (1955). For example, in *London Eats Out: 500 Years of Capital Dining*, we learn that nineteenth-century Londoners could choose from a true cornucopia of street stands and takeout shops, including whelks in barrels, penny ham sandwiches, baked potatoes, Italian ice cream, hot pies, and hot eels (Ehrman et al. 1999: 84–85). Going back still earlier, historian Beat Kumin reports that "By the late Middle Ages, a dense network of inns existed throughout most of Europe," and such eateries provided a considerable amount of catering and takeout services (2003: 71). In Japan, quick and cheap soba (buckwheat) noodle shops serving city workers date back at least to the mid-seventeenth century – as do roving street stands selling tempura and grilled eel (Pilcher 2006b: 40). The demand for convenience may well be nearly universal, or at least a function of "civilization" (Latin for urbanized society). "City people have been busy and pressed for time since the first cities of ancient Mesopotamia," Richard Wilk notes (2006: 193).

Moreover, not all women are or were good cooks. The fact is that we don't really know how many women liked cooking or were good at it. Food memoirs, cookbooks, and even food studies textbooks are largely written by and for those who do cook – or at least think they should. Many classic cookbooks have been written by women aspiring to get *out* of the kitchen to pursue more public careers. Lydia Child used profits from *The Frugal Housewife* (1829) – one of the most popular guides of the mid-nineteenth century – to finance abolitionist projects (Haber 2004: 230). Catherine Beecher preached bourgeois domesticity in *Treatise on Domestic Economy* (1841) but stayed single and lectured widely about social issues throughout her life (Ross 2004: 74). Ellen Richards, who urged that homemade soups would keep men out of saloons, was MIT's first female doctoral student – and a member of its chemistry faculty until she died in 1911 (Shapiro 1986).

The proliferation of cookbooks since early modern times can also be interpreted as a reflection of culinary inexperience, if not also incompetence – otherwise why so much reliance on outside advice? Historian Jessamyn Neuhaus writes that while cookbooks "might demonstrate what people ate, they can easily portray what people wished they could eat" (2003: 3). Similarly, much of food history focuses on the ornamental haute cuisine of elites who could hire *others* to do their cooking.

And the greatest prestige in that arena went to male *chefs*, not female *cooks*, who were considered inferior kitchen workers. Hence the long-standing stereotype that French *cuisine* (male) was inferior to English *cooking* (female) (Mennell 1996: 200–14).

As with so much of social history, we know little about life at the grass roots and in the kitchen. Inarticulate women may have used food as a "voice," but unless they wrote their culinary "songs" down, we don't have a record of what and how they cooked. We do have suggestive hints of trouble in domestic paradise, however. Take the old Irish song about "Mrs. Murphy's Chowder," which contained, among other things, "Meatballs, fish balls, mothballs, cannonballs ..." Another variant, "Who Put the Trousers in Mrs. Murphy's Chowder?" acknowledged that not all festive meals turned out as savory as Hank Williams's jambalaya. Perhaps appropriately, novelist Mark Winegardner introduces his collection of food memoirs, *We Are What We Ate* (1998) with a rather grim recollection of his mother's trailer park cooking, which generally entailed slapping a half-thawed pound of hamburger in a skillet and then, while the meat fried, figuring out whether to add Campbell's Cream of Mushroom soup, Kraft mac 'n' cheese, or canned tuna. (Of Proust's paean to a "decoction of lime flowers," Winegardner observes: "You go, Marcel. Me, I had to look up 'decoction' in the dictionary ... I'm pretty sure nobody in my family ever decocted anything, unless Jell-O counts" (1998: 8). Another author in the same collection quotes Nelson Algren's dictum, "Never eat at a place called Mom's," and recalls his own mother's "cuisine of simulation. We embraced replacement foods. We drank Kool-Aid instead of juice. Oleo was cheaper than butter ... Our gastronomic philosophy was, *Look, you eat or you die, so let's just get it over with and get on living*" (Dufresne 1998: 82–83). In *Tender at the Bone*, restaurant critic Ruth Reichl recalls that her mother was "the queen of mold," whose attempts at home-cooked breakfast tasted somewhere between "cat toes" and "antique anchovies." Perhaps foreshadowing her future role as primary culinary gatekeeper for the *New York Times* and *Gourmet*, the young Reichl's mission "was to keep Mom from killing anybody who came to dinner" (1998: 3–5). While the "art of culinary disaster" has been celebrated and spoofed at the Museum of Burnt Food website,[8] one can also detect serious resistance, if not downright aggression, in Marge Piercy's poem, "What's that smell in the kitchen?" which starts: "All over America women are burning dinner ..." (Avakian 1997: 111).

Of "home cooking" feminist Charlotte Perkins Gilman quipped in 1903, "The long-suffering human system (perhaps toughened by ages of home cooking) will adapt itself even to slow death" (Gilman 1972: 125). That women needed to be freed from domestic reproductive roles was clear enough to many early twentieth-century reformers, who avidly proposed a variety of arrangements, ranging from good takeout services and cooperative housekeeping, to synthetic foods and meals in a pill. For Gilman, professionally prepared food was more "evolved" and would elevate "popular taste. We should acquire a cultivated appreciation of what *is* good food, far removed from the erratic and whimsical self-indulgence of the private table. Our only standard of taste in cooking is personal appetite and caprice. That we 'like' a dish is enough to warrant full approval. But liking is only adaptation" (Gilman 1966: 250). Going several steps further, populist agitator Mary E. Lease predicted in 1893 that within a hundred years agricultural science would allow us "to take, in condensed form from the rich loam of the earth, the life force or germs now found in the heart of the corn, in the kernel of wheat, and in the luscious juice of the fruits. A small phial of this life from the fertile bosom of Mother Earth will furnish men with substance for days. And thus the problems of cooks and cooking will be solved" (Belasco 2006a: 27–28).

Likewise, other nineteenth-century feminist utopians pointed to the need to do something to save the "roasted lady at the head of the table," and perhaps also to reduce reliance on the incompetent "Bridget" [Irish cook] whose purported tendency to burn dinner would not have surprised Piercy. In Anna Dodd's 1887 satirical novel about New York in 2050, *The Republic of the Future*, pneumatic tubes deliver prescription bottles of food tablets directly to kitchen-less apartments. "When the last pie was made into the first pellet," Dodd's narrator explains, "women's true freedom began" (Belasco 2006a: 116–117). Although the meal pill never came to fruition, Bolsheviks did introduce public, communal dining rooms soon after the Russian Revolution in part, historian Mauricio Borrero writes, to "free women from the tyranny of the home kitchen, where they spent long hours preparing food for their families." For Lenin, such experiments in state-sponsored dining served "as living examples of small-deeds communism in practice" (Borrero 2002: 269). In the capitalist version, fast food restaurants offered some of the relief originally envisioned by feminist utopians. For example, in "Home to McDonald's: Upholding the Family Dinner with the Help of McDonald's," ethnologist Helene Brembeck argues that in addition to relieving women of some cooking and cleaning chores, fast food meals *can* be more egalitarian and family-friendly than those at home, where more routine hierarchies and stresses prevail (2005).

Yet while modern women – communist and capitalist alike – now employ many laborsaving technologies, products, and services, they have resisted a complete socialization of cooking. Although the 1950s have been termed the "golden age of food processing" in which marketers launched a full-scale assault on scratch cooking, (Levenstein 1993: 101–118), Laura Shapiro writes that "Cooking, it turned out, had roots so deep and stubborn that even the mighty fist of the food industry couldn't yank them up" (2004: xxiv). Even as women avidly purchased processed foods and followed recipes in Peg Bracken's best-selling *I Hate to Cook Cookbook*

(1960), they also relished Irma Rombauer's ode to the kitchen, *Joy of Cooking* (1931) and Julia Child's smash best-seller, *Mastering the Art of French Cooking* (1961). As a compromise, they may have tried the recipe for "Eight-Can Casserole" in the Oakland [Iowa] Centennial Cookbook (1982), or even have submitted an "original" recipe combining boxed cake mixes, canned almond slivers, ersatz whipped cream, and crushed candy bars to the hugely popular Pillsbury Bake-Off (Stern 1984: 274). In fact women have long incorporated newfangled foods into their "home cooking," and when one considers that tomatoes, chili peppers, chocolate, corn, and potatoes came to most of the world only after 1492, it's hard to draw a clear line between the "traditional" and "modern." "All food is creative in some way, and grounded in the past in other ways," anthropologist Wilk observes (2006: 194).

This apparent contradiction probably results from an intense negotiation among all three points of the triangle: a respect for food's powerful voice (identity), a healthy suspicion of distant, impersonal providers (the responsibility issue), and the higher cost of packaged or professionally prepared food (the convenience issue). The reluctance to give up on what Shapiro calls the "emotional economy" of the kitchen even as the majority of women serve as both producers and consumers in the public "cash economy" (2004: xxiii) suggests a profound ambivalence – and also helps to maintain the notorious "second shift," in which women essentially work two jobs a day. Along with the challenges of multiple jobs, increased expectations for food quality and creativity have raised the stress level in many kitchens, where cooks may find themselves having to perform before an ever more discriminating audience of family and guests (Julier 2004).

A similar complexity surrounds the food–sex nexus, and as above, these divided feelings are reflected in popular food songs. On the one hand women may value their role as empowered makers of labor-intensive festive dishes such as tamales. On the other hand, women find themselves cast as "hot tamales" – objects in innumerable songs of male lust and fear. In "They're Red Hot" (1936), bluesman Robert Johnson both lusts for this "long and tall" woman and also fears that she will "upset your backbone, put your kidneys to sleep." The song was covered in 1991 by the Red Hot Chili Peppers, in "Blood Sugar Sex Magik," a title that appropriately suggested the mixed appeal of such "hot tamales."

Aggressive female sexuality can threaten males – and vice versa. For centuries women have been likened to pieces of meat subject to male predation. The *Dictionary of Historical Slang* lists a variety of meat metaphors for female sex objects: "bit of meat" (a man's first sexual experience), "fresh meat" (a new prostitute), "hot meat" (a loose woman), "raw meat" (a naked woman), "meat market" (prostitute rendezvous place), and "meat house" (brothel) (Fiddes 1991: 150). If women are seen as varieties of meat (chicks, clams, mutton, lamb chops) and their body parts are dissected accordingly (leg, thigh, loin, rump, breast) it is understandable that eating meat might be a problem for some women. Historians of Victorian cuisine have detected a decided female hesitancy, if not antipathy, to eating meat, in part because carnality at the table might also suggest carnality in bed, especially of the violent, non-romantic kind. "Meat is widely reputed to inflame the lustful passions, particularly in men," Nick Fiddes writes, "the stimulation being of an animal rather than of an erotic kind" (147). Thus nineteenth-century vegetarian crusader Sylvester Graham attacked meat and masturbation simultaneously, for both seemed to heighten male sexual energies at the expense of female partners (Wharton 1982, Nissenbaum 1988). For upper-class Anglo-American women of the Victorian era, historian Joan Jacobs Brumberg has shown, the estrangement from meat became quite extreme: "No food (other than alcohol) caused Victorian women and girls greater moral anxiety than meat." For these women at least, being "civilized" meant eating less red meat – a direct contradiction of the prevailing belief that Progress meant eating more beef (the nutrition transition). "Meat eating in excess was linked to adolescent insanity and nymphomania" (1989: 176). Similarly, Laura Shapiro attributes the genteel fetish of the decorative salad to "the assumption that women were averse to red meat." In the most popular late Victorian cookbooks, meat was to be disguised, and even frankfurters were to be blanketed in a "purifying" (and feminizing) white sauce (1986: 91–102).

In her quasi-autobiographical novel *Of Dreams and Assassins*, Algerian-born physician Malika Mokeddem draws an especially graphic link between sexual violence and meat in a sketch of her sexually "voracious" father, a butcher who approached meat and women with the same savagery.

> His obsession [with women] was an ideal activity in an ideal setting: the butcher shop. Between suspended animal carcasses, among swarms of flies, and with the odor of blood he is at ease. Handling meat keeps him ready while he waits for prey. You have to see him grab hold of a large piece of beef or mutton, and with a wrestler's movement, throw it on the butcher block. He grabs an ax and whack! Whack! Whack! Three chops, three breaths. Cut up. He moves away. Fascinated, he observes the scene: gaping cuts, crushed bones ...

Staring at the bloody stains "with an expression of silent amusement bordering on lunacy," he transfers the same predatory gaze to women who enter his shop. "Women are nothing more than meat to him." Completing the connection, he barters meat to seduce the "most destitute of his clientele: a bit of lamb, mutton or camel in exchange for sex. Beef is too expensive" (Mokeddem 2000: 6–7). While meat industry ads claim that beef is "real food for real people," in many cultures only males are considered "real" enough to eat it.

Throughout the world, feminist activist Carol Adams writes, "Meat is a constant for men, intermittent for women" (1992: 26). As an example, Adams cites recent famines in Ethiopia, where starving women were required to prepare two meals, one with animal protein for males, the other without for women. A body of anthropological literature suggests that as Paleolithic male hunters overran wild game, they grabbed the depleted meat supplies for themselves – thus encouraging women to explore and invent horticultural alternatives (Ross 1987: 18). Along similar lines, anthropologist Sidney Mintz observes that while nineteenth-century working-class British men demanded their daily meat ration – much of it shipped from famine-stricken Ireland and Scotland – their wives were getting by on cheap calories from bread, sugar, and jam, which became a mass-produced staple at that time (Mintz 1986: 145; Ross 1987: 30). Reflecting the same dichotomy, American food policy during the Second World War assumed that fighting men deserved red meat, while women could make do with protein substitutes. After the war, historian Amy Bentley (1998) suggests, American women were more favorably disposed to the continuation of meat and flour rationing if it helped to alleviate hunger elsewhere. Even today, persistent under-consumption of meat may exacerbate some chronic "female" conditions such as anemia *if* a diet is not "balanced" in other ways (George 1994). Conversely, male over-consumption of animal protein may contribute to many chronic health problems – a clear example of the conflict between identity (male = meat) and responsibility (long-term health consequences).

In reaction, many feminist reformers have been vegetarians – an ideology also seen in feminist speculative fiction, where calls for more conscientious consumption receive especially sympathetic hearings from ears already attuned to the gender inequities of meat consumption. In the all-female utopia *Mizora*, artificially synthesized meat is considered "a more economical way of obtaining meat than by fattening animals" (Lane 1880: 74). Similarly, in Charlotte Perkins Gilman's *Herland* (1915), eliminating livestock saves space, and the inhabitants are in any case outraged by the idea of eating flesh or robbing a calf of its milk to feed a human. Even the "Creature" in Mary Shelley's *Frankenstein* (1818) becomes a vegetarian when he flees the amoral, paternalistic Victor who created him (Adams 1992: 108–119).

Shunning or critiquing meat has also become a powerful tool in more recent resistance to patriarchy. Perhaps the most well-known analysis is Adams's *Sexual Politics of Meat: A Feminist-Vegetarian Critical Theory* (1992), which finds a clear pattern of male domination in "texts of meat" ranging from the anthropological to the literary, from folktales to military ration recipe books. Accepting the "You are what you eat" paradigm, Adams urges that eating rice (the core staple of many vegetarian diets) is a way of "destabilizing patriarchy" and proclaiming "faith in women" (190). Other activists have adopted a more provocative, *reductio ad absurdum* approach.

For example, in *Sweet Meat*, performance artist Heather Weathers wears a "meat bikini" knit from 30lb of choice beef shoulder. After distributing a flyer decrying "the objectification of women," she models the bikini, then slowly cuts off cubes of meat, which she barbecues for the crowd. Similarly in the 1980s, former fashion model Ann Simonton demonstrated frequently outside beauty pageants wearing a "meat dress" made from skirt steaks, adorned with a necklace of frankfurters, or a bologna and olive loaf number with parsley corsage. Gang-raped as a teenager, Simonton made an even stronger statement (and was arrested for it) at a Miss California contest in Santa Cruz, where she wore a bathing suit made from pork ribs and splashed the hall's steps with her own blood while hostile counter-protesters chanted, "Dress meat, not women."[9]

EMBATTLED FOOD

Looking beyond the gender and meat-related issues, food consumption itself poses major conflicts for many modern people – as seen perhaps in the increase in chronic dieting and, worse, life-threatening food disorders, and not just among women. On the one hand consumers are urged to enjoy themselves through food. After all, eating is very pleasurable – not to mention its utility as a vehicle of self-expression, power, and general sensuality. Consumer culture considers bountiful, tasty food to be an entitlement, a basic component of travel, family and community maintenance, and spicy romance. And thanks to the efficiencies of the globalized, industrial food system, food is more convenient than ever. As omnivores we are programmed to eat a lot, and now that the constraints are off for many (but not most) of us, why *not* eat as much as you want? Indeed, *not* eating can stigmatize individuals and upset social relations – as lone vegetarians discover when dining amongst carnivores. And as sociologist Ashby Walker (2005) finds in her compassionate study of patients with feeding tubes, people who cannot eat "normally" suffer severe identity loss and may become a threat to family cohesiveness. To be human, one *must* eat.

On the other hand, eating too much can obviously have major implications for self-image (identity) as well as personal and environmental health (responsibility). While some traditional cultures value fatness as a sign of affluence and generosity, modern cultures on the whole tend to stigmatize it. "In contemporary North America and Europe," anthropologists Don Kulick and Anne Meneley observe, "the tone with which the word 'fat' is uttered is often concerned, ashamed, alarmist, or condemnatory. Fat, we are told relentlessly, is bad" (2005: 2). Explanations abound for the cult of thinness – a refusal to grow up, a fear of female sexuality itself, a fear of losing control, a proclamation of self-mastery and discipline, a psychobiological disorder, a reaction against oppressive family meals, the result of *not enough* family meals, a perverse admiration for tubercular romantic poets, Puritanism run amok, and so on. Whatever the causes, the fear of fat takes an especially high toll on women for whom *not* eating may communicate "voice." Even those who may not succumb to a disabling food disorder may still find themselves restricting what or how much they eat in front of others – a relic of the genteel Victorian belief that "A woman should never be seen eating" (Brumberg 1989: 164–188). And with the mounting fear that an "obesity epidemic" may outrun modern medicine and bankrupt modern economies, not eating has become a political, medical, and moral imperative. (More on this in Chapter 5.)

In all, it may be time to bury – or at least complicate – the "We are what we eat" axiom. That food has *something* to do with personal and social identity may be the best we can do here. And it's time to get on to the *other* things that food has much to do with – economics, politics, justice, health, and environment.

Chapter Summary

- Food and sex are intimately connected, as can be seen in popular song lyrics.
- Reflecting a heritage of scarcity and poverty, love songs of the early twentieth century were especially rich in food metaphors.
- As food has become more problematic and also more taken for granted in recent decades, the range of eroticized foods in lyrics has narrowed somewhat.
- For women, food can be both a means of empowerment and enslavement, control and oppression.
- Whether female or male, foodwork is strenuous, hot, tedious, repetitive, and often unappreciated.
- Not all moms are good cooks.
- "Convenience" is a long-standing demand. People have been eating prepared, fast food for centuries.
- Historically, meat has been more of a concern for men than for women.
- For some people, *not* eating is an expression of "voice."

4 CONVENIENCE: THE GLOBAL FOOD CHAIN

In Eric Carle's children's classic, *Pancakes, Pancakes!* (1990), young Jack wakes up with a powerful hunger for pancakes. This poses a challenge for Jack's mother, who needs freshly harvested, threshed, and ground flour from the mill, an egg from the black hen, milk from the spotted cow, butter churned from fresh cream, firewood for the stove, jam from the storage shelves, and so on. Eventually – thirty splendid pages and countless hours later – Jack gets his rather plain but well-earned pancake. Delayed gratification yields pedagogical rewards, for Carle's readers get a lesson in the pastoral food chain, including clear illustrations of archaic tools such as flails, threshers, sickles, millstones, axes, churns – a feature very attractive to elementary school teachers who use the book to teach city children about basic food provisioning, preparation, and nutrition. One enterprising fourth-grade teacher even uses it to teach students key economic principles, especially "Consumption; Production; Interdependence; Natural Capital and Human Resources."[1]

The book appeals because most children – and parents – don't know where their food comes from. Indeed, if they eat pancakes at all – a questionable assumption given the time and basic skills involved in making them from scratch, or even from a box – they're more likely to come as part of a McDonald's breakfast, a menu apparently so deserving of the company's slogan, "I'm lovin' it," that customers have actively lobbied the corporation to make it a day-long option. Mindful that the highly profitable breakfast segment is expanding 9 percent a year, McDonald's promises to consider the petition.[2] After all, this is the company that once boasted, "We do it all for you," and "You deserve a break today."

McDonald's founder Ray Kroc was also famous for preaching this basic principle of management, KISS (Keep it Simple, Stupid). In a way, the whole modern industrial food chain does have just one simple product: convenience. In return for a fee, the food industry saves us the time, labor, energy, bother, sweat, strain, skill, and dangers involved in raising, preparing, and sometimes even digesting the ingredients in our pancakes and almost everything else we eat. The global retail food bill for this convenience runs about US$5 trillion a year, half of it sold by stores, the other half by restaurants.[3] In the United States alone, 40,000 supermarkets employed over 3.5 million people and sold US$500 billion worth of food products in 2006. Add to this another 140,000 "convenience stores" such as 7-Eleven.[4] Food service – McDonald's and others – grossed another US$500 billion in the United States, and employed over 10 million workers.[5] Yet despite these enormous revenues, it seems a very simple proposition: we pay others to feed us so we can do other things.

Or is it so simple? Ray Kroc might well have resisted the day-long breakfast menu, as it would entail adding and training staff and finding room for new grills (instead of converting the same grills from pancakes to burgers at lunch). Indeed, Kroc would have preferred no breakfast menu at all. "Breakfast is not as easy as it appears," notes McDonald's current chief operating officer, Ralph Alvarez.[6] In fact, the convenience food supply system is immensely complicated, entailing the closely coordinated efforts of hundreds of millions of people who plant, tend, pick, move, store, chop, cook, wrap, sell, and dispose of our processed plants and livestock – not to mention the many others who work for those who supply the suppliers: the manufacturers of vital "inputs" such as hoes, seeds, agrichemicals, tractors, trucks, refrigerators, paper bags, knives, hamburger/pancake grills, and so on.[7] Most of the "value added" is made far up the food chain from the farm, for just a little over two million Americans were listed as "farm proprietors" in 2002 (most of them not full-time, self-supporting farmers), while 1 million worked in agricultural inputs and servicing (supplying combines, milking machines, etc.), 2.5 million in agricultural processing (converting grain to pancake mixes, cream to butter, etc.) and over 16 million in wholesale and retail food sales.[8] The longer the chain is, the smaller the farmer's share. Reflecting the growing complexity of global commissary, the farmer's share of the food dollar declined from forty cents in 1910 to seven cents in 1997. The rest went to the suppliers and "middlemen," most of them working for mega-corporations such as Archer Daniels Midland and Cargill (who control 75 percent of the world's market for cereals), Nestlé (the world's largest food manufacturer), and Wal-Mart, the largest food retailer in the United States (Halweil 2004: 45–47). Another way of putting it is this: in 2000 the entire "food and fiber system" added over US$1.2 trillion to the US gross domestic product. "Of this, US$757 billion came from manufacturing and distribution, while US$426 billion came from inputs. The farm sector by itself accounted for US$82 billion."[9]

What do we make of all this? Should our reliance on globalized agro-food conglomerates be deplored or celebrated? Some critics view the modern food industry as an agent of our own loss of independence, vigor, knowledge, and competence, rendering us uncomfortably vulnerable to distant decisions and catastrophes. At the very least our demand for convenience suggests a degree of privilege, choice and discretion unavailable to the world's poor. While the value of world agricultural trade quadrupled between 1960 and 2000, to over US$400 billion (Halweil 2004: 9), much of the flow benefited the richest consumers. As an indicator of the inequities in global interdependence, in 2004 the United States imported over US$60 billion in food, much of it luxuries, such as US$3.5 billion worth of wine, US$3.3 billion of beef, US$2 billion in coffee, US$1.2 billion of bananas, and US$740 million in olive oil. Conversely, impoverished Albania imported just US$6 million worth of beef and bananas; even less in coffee, wine, and olive oil. Its top agricultural imports were wheat (US$37 million) and cigarettes (US$30 million).[10]

Moralism also colors this critique. Are we simply too "lazy" to feed ourselves? In this frame, "convenience" is the mark of decadence, exhaustion, and exploitation – a relic of aristocratic indolence and irresponsibility, a correlate of boredom, depression, and corpulence. Who would ever aspire to be poet-farmer Wendell Berry's "passive American consumer, sitting down to a meal of pre-prepared or fast food, ... with inert, anonymous substances that have been processed, dyed, breaded, sauced, gravied, ground, pulped, strained, blended, prettified, and sanitized beyond resemblance to any part of any creature that ever lived"? (1989: 127). Enamored of "'effortless' shopping from a list of available goods on a television monitor and heating precooked food by remote control," such "industrial eaters" are simply ignorant, irresponsible, and easily deceived. A convenience food system "implies, and indeed depends on a perfect ignorance of the history of the food that is consumed. It requires that the citizenry should give up their hereditary and sensible aversion to buying a pig in a poke" (126). The fact that most modern urban readers will not know the meaning of "a pig in a poke"[11] may prove Berry's point.

In a similar vein, historian William Cronon argues that the meat industry – pioneer in so many aspects of modern food processing and marketing – depends on consumer "forgetfulness," an almost intentional obliviousness to the violence of the slaughterhouse (Cronon 1991: 256). In the populist agrarian worldview of educator David Orr, the pursuit of short-term convenience pushes us "toward a kind of insensate high-tech barbarism," with a consequent loss of traditional "moral and civic virtue" (1994: 174). Such moralization may also extend to the way one culture stereotypes and stigmatizes another. When sociologist Christy Shields-Argelès asked 176 French respondents what they thought of American cuisine, most replied "McDonald's" or "Fast food," which they characterized with such negatives as "uniform," "unbalanced," "gobbled up," "artificial," and "no taste." In gastronomic terms at least, few had anything positive to say about "the Anglo-Saxon Other," whose globalized convenience food was now seen as a clear threat to French autonomy and traditions (Shields-Argelès 2004: 18–20). And with fast food, supermarket, and convenience store outlets proliferating throughout the world, and even in France, the barbarians were clearly at the gates.

When Shields-Argelès asked 167 Americans what they thought of their own food, however, the descriptions were far more favorable: "Plenty of choice," "Anything you want," "Abundance," "All the variety you can find in the whole world," and, thanks to faith in government regulation, "Free from diseases" (20–21). While some American respondents did agree with the negative views voiced by Berry, Orr, and the French, most felt quite comfortable with their options. And why shouldn't we celebrate the efficiency and ingenuity of a system that feeds so many people so cheaply? After all, whereas the average American family spent about 46 percent of its income on food in 1901, by 1995 it was 14 percent, and under 10 percent after 2004. Even less was spent for food at home: 6.1 percent, with much of the affluent world following close after: the United Kingdom 8.3 percent, Germany 10.9 percent, and Japan 13.4 percent. Even the French – said to value food more highly than Americans – spent just 13.6 percent, which is twice the American average but still quite low compared to other countries and times. Reflecting the relative poverty of their economies, consumers in Mexico spend nearly a quarter (24 percent) of their disposable income on food at home, and about half in India (48.4 percent) and the Philippines (52.9 percent).[12] Even more remarkable are the food industry's productivity gains, achieved primarily through the use of convenient, labor-saving technologies – especially better seeds, fertilizers, tractors, sprinklers, harvesters, tools, and trucks – as well as more efficient systems of manufacturing and marketing (again, pioneered by the meat industry). In 1900 it took about 37 percent of the American labor force, working on 5.7 million farms, to feed 76 million people; by 2005 less than 2.5 percent of the workforce labored on 2 million farms to feed 300 million people – with another US$60 billion in agricultural products left over for export.[13] In contrast, over 60 percent of India's population still works in agriculture, and yet almost 50 percent of its children are considered undernourished.[14]

Moreover, isn't this what human creativity is all about? Humans "come together" (the root of "convenience" is *convenir* as in "convene") to devise countless ingenious devices, relationships, and institutions in the relentless pursuit of "utility," which Enlightenment philosophers and economists termed the "law of least action" – the desire to get maximum output for minimum input (Manuel 1965: 67). And what's wrong with being comfortable? According to Francis Bacon (1561–1626), late Renaissance era patron saint of utopian engineers and technologists, the role of science is "to make imperfect man comfortable."[15] In this view, the demand for convenience becomes the engine of Progress not just at home but throughout society. Human attention spans are limited; we all have "attention deficit disorder." If we spend our time thinking about how to grow, gather, and prepare food, we have less attention to devote to other tasks; having spent his morning making pancakes, Jack had little time or energy left for physics or piano. But if we are freed from having to pay attention to where our food comes from, we can pay attention to other endeavors, some trivial (reading about Paris Hilton), some not (saving the planet). According to this emancipatory argument, modern laborsaving conveniences liberated peasants from feudal oppression and enabled the relatively few remaining farmers to read, travel, and send their children to college. Displaced farmers became urban factory workers who produced more goods for more people – the consumer revolution. When feminism surged in the late 1960s, influential nutritionist Jean Mayer applied the same rhetoric of deliverance: "The women's liberation movement became possible when labor-saving devices freed adult females from many of the drudgeries of housekeeping. Refrigerators eliminated the need for daily food shopping, modern stoves and dishwashers reduced somewhat the time associated with the preparation of meals. The development of convenience foods, however, was the major quantum jump in freeing the housewife from the need of spending hours every day being the family cook" (quoted in Belasco 2006b: 124). Similar arguments have been mustered to explain the fall of communism, the antiwar movement, environmentalism, and even consumer protests against modern food – all made possible, industry defenders assert, by the abundance, security, and free time afforded by labor-saving, mass-produced goods and services. In this frame, the modern food industry takes on the familiar mantle of the humble servant making life convenient for the master, only now the master is the ordinary citizen, not the decadent aristocrat (Belasco 2006b: 122–126).

So is convenience good or bad? As with all such dichotomies, the answer is mixed. Yes, we should celebrate such a system that brings so much food to so many people, but we should also question it, if for no other reason than self-protection. Something as big and vital as the food industry certainly deserves close scrutiny and skepticism. Human societies have always paid extra attention to those who provision the citizenry – often granting special privileges to hunters, bakers, butchers, cooks, and so on, in return for the right to inspect, regulate, and control how food is distributed. Why should McDonald's, Tesco, or Delhaize be any different?

But before we get to evaluating it, we need to understand it – and given its size and distance, that's hard. To be blunt, the food industry is not especially "transparent" about its sources and practices. Ask anyone who has attempted to find out where a particular ingredient comes from. Students who naively email or phone corporate public relations departments for basic production and marketing information rarely come back with more than a few recipes and maybe a discount coupon. Food industry websites are not much more forthcoming, as they exist primarily to put the best spin on company activities. For a self-styled "servant" to public needs and fancies, the food industry can be even more sullen and incommunicative than the Victorian aristocracy's downstairs "help."

One way to illuminate and demystify the supply chain is to write a history of a single foodstuff. Such studies often highlight the unappreciated importance and influence of common foods, such as the potato (Salaman 1949), cod (Kurlansky 1997), sugar (Mintz 1986), salt (Kurlansky 2002), tomatoes (Smith 1994), peanuts (Smith 2002), oysters (Kurlansky 2006), and bananas (Jenkins 2000; Soluri 2005). Culinary historians have also provided useful sketches of more prepared foods, such as marmalade (Wilson 1999), popcorn (Smith 2001), Coca-Cola (Pendergast 2000), the Twinkie (Ettlinger 2007), or of a complete meal, whether home cooked (Visser 1986) or fast food (Rozin 1994). From a reader's standpoint, these books have the advantage of being tightly focused and usually relate a satisfying narrative of a food's social, political, and economic maturation – often with the built-in drama of the Ugly Duckling/Cinderella variety: a once scorned dish becomes belle of the ball. But quite often they are strongest on the origins and traditional uses of these foods – rather than their current business and cultural context, which may be ephemeral and difficult to nail down, except perhaps in a perfunctory final chapter. Moreover, in celebrating their particular foods, some tend towards hyperbole and simplistic determinism – finding a bit too much influence and power in a particular ingredient. History is far too complex and unknowable to be governed by a single condiment, however important.

Another way to find out where our food comes from is commodity chain analysis, which seeks to trace the path of food as it moves through the global supply system, from field to table, plant to plate (and sometimes beyond to the dump). It certainly borrows heavily on the information unearthed by the writers cited above, but its focus is more contemporary, its tools more multidisciplinary. Such study identifies the actors and agents, institutions and arrangements, technologies, resources, and values that come together (again, *convenir*) to provision us. Technically, in biological terms, such combinations constitute more of a "food web" than a "food chain," which is shorter and more linear – no more than 4–5 "links" in the transformation of solar energy to edible calories. Our food system is vastly more complicated, and often quite unnatural. In a biological food chain, energy is lost at every stage, while in our corporate food chain, extra energy – often in petrochemical form – is actually added along the way, from fertilizing plants and fueling irrigation pumps in the field to powering trucks and forklifts at the store. According to Michael Pollan, our food industry uses up ten calories for every single calorie made available for consumption (2006: 183). The longer the chain, the more energy expended along the way. (More on this in Chapter 6.)

But even if the provisioning system is not, strictly speaking, a "chain," that term does have some conceptual use in helping us to visualize and investigate the scope of system. At the very least it helps us know where to look, and which disciplinary tools might be helpful.[16]

For example, most obviously, there are *chain stores and restaurants* – elaborate institutional arrangements designed to maximize convenience, economies of scale, and profits, while minimizing interactions, competition, and consumer consciousness. Along these lines, the thesaurus offers synonyms such as syndicates, cartels, combines, conglomerates, and trusts. Studying this aspect of food chains entails a risky and possibly subversive look at the consolidation and execution of corporate power; hence the relative lack of transparency.

For labor and business studies, there are also the "chains" of *bondage* – the steely shackles that bind farmers to bugs and weather, workers to bosses, manufacturers to consumers, household cooks to picky children and partners. One can also think about *chain gangs* and *chains of command*. Studying these chains means examining the many human orders, obligations, incentives, deals, and restraints that shape the movement of food from field to fork. Here again, we are examining the exercise of influence and power.

For students of sociological distinction, status, and stratification, there are *chain-link fences*: tools and institutions that divide insiders and outsiders, the privileged and the disposed. Such barriers, hedges, railings, and screens determine who gets dinner and who doesn't. Here we get into issues of class, food security, and obesity.

For ecologists, there are *chain reactions*: the downstream, domino effects of seemingly innocuous actions, such as the piece of toast in Minneapolis that breaks the levees in New Orleans. And peering upstream, there are *genetic chains*, the tiny strands that archive the results of the millions of breeding experiments that produced the tasty ingredients in today's dinner.

For psychologists of consumption, there are *chain smokers*: people addicted to repetitive, compulsive, potentially self-destructive behavior that extends beyond tobacco to many drug foods, including sugar, fat, salt, caffeine, and alcohol. Along the same lines, there is Aretha Franklin's *chain of fools* – people who get hooked by the cruel seducers but who vow to break the links one day and move on. Chains can bind us, but as Aretha notes, they also have weak links.

For moralists such as David Orr or the late David Brower of the Sierra Club, Friends of the Earth, and Earth Island Institute, there's our unsustainably speculative "*chain letter economy*, in which we pick up early handsome dividends and our children find their mailboxes empty" (Brower quoted in McPhee 1971: 82). To what extent is the current food system an elaborate Ponzi scheme, a speculative bubble or pyramid, in which, for the sake of low prices and high fat, we're squandering our children's inheritance?

Clearly, there are many difficult issues here. Tackling them requires considerable organization and discipline.[17] In my own capstone undergraduate research seminar, "The American Food Chain," students select one food product to trace and then are guided through a multi-stage process of investigation and analysis, leading eventually to 5,000-word final reports on diverse products such as oatmeal, Jell-O, instant couscous, low-fat yogurt drinks, Diet Coke, table grapes, and Ben & Jerry's ice cream. Short exercises break down the task into small steps, the first of which is to develop an intimate relationship with the product by describing its appearance, taste, feel, and smell, noting also the design of its packaging and the significance of its brand name. Another exercise addresses the nutritional composition and controversies associated with the product. Ingredients are listed, additives defended, subtractives (the things taken out) deplored. Students then select the one or two most important and interesting ingredients to trace back to the field. Exercises on agriculture and processing identify the primary sources of these foods, how they are produced, where, and by whom, the farmer's relationships with wholesalers and distributors, and the conditions of farm and factory workers. Then comes an exercise on marketing, the comprehensive process by which products are packaged, segmented, priced, displayed, and pitched. And finally, students must consider the consumer: who uses the product and why? How does this product serve the identity and community-building functions analyzed in Chapters 2 and 3? How is the food prepared, eaten, discussed, and disposed of? Why might it be hard to give up (a question often overlooked by moralists decrying consumer "laziness" and self-indulgence)? In all these areas, students are encouraged to look for the conflicts and controversies that give the story some narrative "crunch."

Box 4.1. Commodity Chain Analysis

Here are some examples of the types of questions addressed in a research exercise in which students trace a single foodstuff's travels and "costs" through the food chain, from farm to plate.

Agriculture

- Where are the principal ingredients grown or raised? (You may have to focus on just a few.)
- Describe and explain the means by which these ingredients are grown. Pay particular attention to the role of agricultural technology (machines, chemicals, irrigation, genetics) and labor (farmers, peasants, migrants, workers). Detail the environmental issues associated with raising this food.
- Who grows this food — small farmers, corporate agribusiness? How much does the farmer make? What percentage of the retail price goes to the farmer?

Processing

- Detail the steps by which raw ingredients from the farm are transformed into the food product we buy in the supermarket or restaurant.
- How do processors attempt to extend the product's shelf life (i.e., preservatives, canning, packaging, freezing, etc.)? What resources are used in order to extend shelf life and where do those resources come from (e.g., electricity requires coal or oil, packaging comes from trees or oil, etc.)?
- Which companies do this processing? What else do they make? Who owns and runs these companies? How profitable are they?

Marketing and Distribution

- How does the product get from processor to retailer?
- How is the final product packaged, advertised, displayed, and priced?
- Who sells the product? What kind of company is this?
- How are store employees treated?
- What health claims are made in the labeling and/or advertising? Are they legitimate? Who are the principal purchasers of this product?
- Analyze the advertising for images, myths, values, gender issues, stereotypes, etc.

Consumption

- Who uses this product, how, and why? Who doesn't use it and why?
- What is the role of this food in the life of the family, community, ethnic group, region, nation?
- To what extent do people use this food because it is "convenient"? What *is* a "convenience food" and how does the demand for convenience relate to wider trends in our society?

Some Ethical and Environmental Questions

- Is this product "safe" to eat? Is it "good for me"?
- Could you sleep at night if you were responsible for growing, processing, or selling this food?
- Is this product *sustainable*? In other words, does eating this product now hurt our grandchildren later?
- Are there better ways to get this food, or should we just give it up?

These are challenging questions. Where can inexperienced, unfunded researchers go for answers? While company websites are by design slanted and self-interested, there are numerous other sources that can be accessed from any library portal, or even one's home computer. To be sure, such sources must be examined with the same skepticism and rigor as any interview, document, or statistic, but at the very least they point investigators toward issues of health, equity, and power that might never have occurred to them given their everyday distance from much of the food chain. Universities, consumer groups, environmental activists, government agencies, think tanks, and international non-governmental organizations maintain informative sites that track pesticides, rural development, farm and factory labor, alternative agriculture, food advertising, nutrition, "food miles," corporate consolidation, and so on. The US Department of Agriculture alone maintains dozens of encyclopedic sites open to all, as does every state college of agriculture, nutrition, human ecology, natural resources business, and public health. To suit growing consumer interest in "green" (environmentally friendly) goods, many sites rate products not only on their environmental impact but also on how they treat workers and home communities.

Students can learn much from the work of best-selling investigative journalists patrolling the food chain (for example, Pollan 2006, Schlosser 2001, Ettlinger 2007). Reading the footnotes in such books can offer a powerful jump-start to the project. It is also possible to piggyback the research of students at other universities. At St Cloud State University in Minnesota, students in Sociology and the Politics of Food have posted enlightening "fact and action" sheets on a wide variety of common products, including shrimp, tobacco, tomatoes, eggs, peanut butter, and beer. These handy briefing papers offer background information on the growth of the industry, news on labor conditions, "Ten things every consumer should know," "Five things you can do," and links to other information resources.[18] And while the industry itself tends to be quite opaque and defensive when it comes to discussing environmental, health, and labor questions, it is much more open in discussing what its customers seem to want (and don't want); such market research can offer invaluable insights into consumer behavior and values. This data can be supplemented by other consumption information gleaned from websites devoted to the anthropology and history of food, personal culinary blogs, and, of course, recipes.

In the final, long version of their study my own students also address two related ethical questions. First, could they sleep at night working for the companies that sell this product? Second, is the product sustainable, and if not is there a better way to get it? (That is, given all that is involved in raising this food and getting it to the table, can we keep producing and consuming it without robbing future generations of resources and opportunities?) Sometimes the answers to both can be very disquieting. After an investigation of seemingly innocuous oatmeal, Sutton Stokes suggested that, behind the benign image of the trademark Quaker stood a company whose pursuit of the cheapest supply of oats threatened the health of rural communities and supported the growth of Cargill, a major force behind "the race to the bottom: ... greater consolidation of farms with a tendency toward unsustainable monoculture, reductions in protections for workers and the environment, and so on." Weighing the product's environmental and social costs against its rather modest nutritional benefits, he concluded that Quaker's extravagant health claims might be taken with the same "dash of salt" recommended on the product's packaging (Stokes 2005: 88–91). Similarly, Mary Potorti found that behind the apparently wholesome – or at least relatively harmless – façade of Jell-O, "Bill Cosby's favorite dessert," lurks a controversial record of deceptive advertising, labor conflict, and environmental pollution, the last mainly due to the nasty processes by which animal byproducts are rendered into gelatin. "While many proudly tout the merits of capitalism as a fundamental aspect of Americanism," Potorti concluded, "the corporate climate that has emerged in today's age of media and consolidation has diminished the integrity of many mass-produced products ... Perhaps then Jell-O *is* the All-American food, for it is generally no better or worse than the system that produces it. In truth Kraft [maker of Jell-O] and others are far smarter than many are willing to acknowledge, for they know the secret that keeps the processed foods industry profitable: Americans will eat just about anything. That is, of course, as long as they don't know what it is" (Potorti 2006: 27). And even the so-called "green" capitalists Ben & Jerry offered little solace for Emily Hunter, who found that the premium ice cream company's sale to multinational conglomerate Unilever signaled that "It is perhaps American to sell out, to put profits first, to use social issues to market to a niche consumer base. In a capitalist society, we know where business values lie, and Ben & Jerry's – despite all their purported hippy ethics – are no exception" (Hunter 2006: 32).

In his classic work on sugar, *Sweetness and Power*, anthropologist Sidney Mintz 1986: 151–158) writes of two very different types of "meaning": the view from inside and the view from outside. The inside view entails looking at what a product means to the people who produce and consume it. How do they use, justify, and think about what they are doing? In his own case Mintz explored the meal practices, beliefs, artistic expression, and iconography that accompanied the expanding use of sugar after the fifteenth century. Examples include the new popularity of wedding cakes, sweetened tea, and the new dependence of the working classes on toast with jam for cheap calories. The outside meaning involves a greater distance, as it asks what it all signifies from the standpoint of long-term political and social systems of power. For Mintz this entailed looking at how sugar production affected the growth of European empires, furthered the unequal distribution of global wealth, and fueled the rise of industrial capitalism.

In my own course, the question about sustainability is basically an outside question: How does this all add up for humanity, both present and future? What does the industrial food chain "mean" for global warming, the state of public health, the distribution of resources, the fate of our grandchildren? We will address that question more fully in the following two chapters. But the first question – "Can you sleep at night?" – is an inside question, as it puts the observer in the subjective position of being a participant in the food chain. How do food producers and marketers see their roles, and what do consumers think about the foods they buy?

There are various ways to get inside the heads of food industry players. Given the populist/agrarian longings of postmodern culture, agricultural workers probably get the most attention. The literature and filmography on slaves, migrant workers, peasants, and yeomen farmers is vast. For insights into the experiences of new-convert organic farmers there are countless memoirs of the "I tried living on the land for a while and then wrote a book about it" variety. People actually making a living in the business rarely have time to write books, however. For their story, we can turn to academic rural sociologists and agricultural historians, who do focus on the plight and challenges facing conventional farmers, but their works are not always access-ible to students or general readers.[19] For starters, here again investigative journalists may be helpful, especially if they can win the trust of the people they are observing and keep their own opinions to themselves. In *Portrait of a Burger as a Young Calf* (2002) Peter Lovenheim apprentices himself to a New York dairy farm for a year. Suspending judgment and qualms, Lovenheim comes to sympathize with these hard-working dairymen who sincerely love their animals even as they send them to slaughter, which is the fate not only of "useless" male calves but of their aging mothers as well.[20] The ambivalence and compassion of Lovenheim's "portrait" may be more believable and compelling for students than Eric Schlosser's muckraking *Fast Food Nation* (2001), which takes a much blunter, outsider approach to the animal industry. While Schlosser's sense of *outrage* (itself a word connoting an outsider's distance) is merited when exposing the industry's safety problems, his most moving chapters may be those that attempt to see the economic dilemmas faced from the inside perspective of beleaguered ranchers and meat workers. Students facing the competing pressures of work and study, careerism and enlightenment, family and freedom, are well equipped to appreciate the stories of people who "do what they have to do." The master of such storytelling may well be John McPhee, who skillfully and poetically enters a very wide range of heads – from orange growers, fishermen, produce farmers at New York City's Greenmarket, and Scottish crofters (peasant farmers), to geologists, land developers, river barge operators, and a Nevada cattle brand inspector.[21]

Compassion tends to diminish as one moves up the corporate food chain. Migrant workers and hardscrabble farmers receive the most sensitive attention. Frontline chefs –especially those working in high-end gourmet restaurants – are the subject of numerous memoirs, films, TV shows, and even an entire cable network, though their portrayal is often more sensationalistic than compassionate. But the people who staff the offices of agri-food suppliers, processors, and major retailers remain largely anonymous, if not serving as stock villains in anti-business melo-dramas. One notable exception is *Lords of the Harvest: Biotech, Big Money, and the Future of Food* (2001), in which reporter Daniel Charles does an excellent job of revealing the idealistic aspirations, bureaucratic constraints, public prejudices, and laboratory disappointments shaping the high-pressured experiences of genetic engineers working for Monsanto. Unlike some outside depictions of Monsanto's workers as mad scientists in the Frankenstein mode, Charles's subjects come across as flesh and blood professionals who hope to do good *and* well – that is, to feed humanity while also making a respectable living. Their internal conflicts between the dictates of pure science and profit-driven expediency are the stuff of modern corporate tragedy. Somewhat similarly, but with much thicker theoretical complexity, anthropologist Theodore Bestor's *Tsukiji: The Fish Market at the Center of the World* (2004) offers a rich insight into the mindset, traditions, contradictions, and dilemmas of Japanese wholesalers working in the world's largest seafood market.

INSIDE GIGANTIC

Business schools often employ elaborate role-play exercises as a way to prepare budding executives for the maelstrom of real world decision-making. In my own undergraduate survey, we conduct an in-class simulation that attempts to capture some of the challenges and conflicts involved in developing food new products. Students also write up their results as individual papers.

While all these questions and criteria may not be exactly how the real world works, they do establish a sense of limits, contradictions, and pressure. While an outside perspective sees a rather oligopolistic market structure – relatively few competitors – from inside the competition among conglomerates can seem intense, e.g., Pepsi vs. Coca-Cola, McDonald's vs. Burger King, Philip Morris vs. Unilever. Acquired companies (such as Gigantic) often face severe budgetary restrictions on what they can spend for ingredients and research. While the list of supplies in Gigantic's Baltimore warehouse may be somewhat implausible, it does convey the lesson that manufacturers usually seek out the cheapest sources, often from distant places. Through a process of "decommodification," just a few cents' worth of simple materials are converted into a US$3.79 "meal," most of its price constituting "value added" somewhere between field and fork. The line extension requirement also addresses a matter of expediency: because it is much cheaper and easier to elaborate an existing item than to devise an entirely original one, line extensions comprise the majority of "new and improved" products.

Much of the challenge of new product development comes from the limits set by consumers themselves, or rather by the consumers as *perceived* by market researchers

Box 4.2. The New Product Development Game

Background

You are the new product development team for the Gigantic Food Corporation, a newly acquired division of the Carcinogenic Tobacco Company. Your principal competitors are Kraft–General Foods–Nabisco, Unilever, and Stouffer's (Nestlé). As the smallest and most ambitious of the major food processors, Gigantic would like to be ultra-aggressive in developing new products, but since Carcinogenic just went heavily into debt to acquire you for US$50 billion (in its attempt to diversify away from cigarettes), you do have a rather limited budget for R&D (research and development) and marketing (advertising, promotions, sales).

Ingredients

With its limited budget, Gigantic must make do with the following supplies currently warehoused in Baltimore:

- Canned string beans and pineapple chunks (from Mexico).
- Frozen ground beef (from Costa Rica).
- Dehydrated potato sticks (from Idaho).
- Dried mushroom bits (from Pennsylvania).
- Extra-light olive oil (from Turkey).
- Textured vegetable protein, like the stuff in Baco's (from Brazilian soybeans).
- High-fructose corn syrup (from Iowa, Illinois).
- Monosodium glutamate and ascorbic acid (from New Jersey).
- Food Dye Blue #2 (from West Virginia).
- Dehydrated garlic, onion, parsley, dill, rosemary (from California).
- Milk powder and processed American cheese (USDA surplus from Wisconsin).
- Modified cornstarch (Iowa).
- Enriched wheat flour (from Argentina).

Marketing Guidelines

- It should retail for under US$3.79 per serving.
- Target customer demographics: age 24–49, metropolitan, household income of US$70,000+.
- It must lend itself to line extension later on, i.e., "new and improved" variations of the theme. For example: Cheerios = basic line; Honey Nut Cheerios = line extension.
- It must fit the fast food formula (see page 69).

The class divides into smaller teams and follows these instructions:

1. Spend at least twenty minutes on the engineering challenge: Design and name a microwaveable product, making sure that all ingredients are used. Design the package, too. Then elect an engineering manager to present your ideas and package in class.
2. Then spend another twenty minutes on the marketing challenge:
   (a) Outline how the product fulfills the fast food formula (see below or page 69).
   (b) Design a television commercial, and a print ad introducing your product.
   (c) Plan the line extension.
   (d) Elect a marketing manager to present in class.
3. Finally, spend another 20 minutes rationalizing your ethical positions, specifically:
   (a) How can you sleep at night knowing that your work is enriching a tobacco company?
   (b) What might Wendell Berry (see page 57) say about your use of distant ingredients, and how would you respond?
   (c) What might Eric Schlosser (*Fast Food Nation*) say about your use of ground beef, and how would you respond?
   (d) What might a cardiologist say about the *product's nutritional profile?*
   (e) Elect an ethics manager to present these positions.

and then discussed in food trade journals. Food marketers set both quantitative and qualitative boundaries on their target market. Quantitatively they tend to seek out busy urban and suburban consumers whose income puts them in the upper 40 percent or so of households. These are the people whose neighborhoods are most saturated with supermarkets and restaurants and who are most able to afford ready-made or microwaveable meals. In return for their patronage, these consumers have complex, often conflicting requirements – as summarized in the "Eight Fs," which originated in roadside, fast food businesses of the 1920s such as Howard Johnson's and White Tower (Belasco 1979, 2001, Hirshorn and Izenour 1979), but which now guide much takeout and convenience food marketing as well. Note that while I am specifically discussing the US market here, to a certain extent these provisos apply wherever modern, American-style cuisine takes root – with some important exceptions to be noted later in the discussion of "glocalization."

THE EIGHT FS

FAMILY

Ever since Americans took to the road en masse in the 1920s, fast food has had to appeal to the whole family. And today, as busy Americans cook at home less, they look for places that can substitute for the family dining room. Food must not be too spicy for children, or too expensive for middle-class budgets. Restrooms must be clean and accessible, the dining area generally bright and airy, like a suburban eat-in kitchen. Plastic tables ease the cleaning up after restless children, who may sometimes be directed to special play areas. Food is generally served by women – surrogate moms or big sisters. In line with middle-class notions of propriety, "family restaurants" rarely serve liquor and never have separate bars. Similarly, takeout convenience products tend to be bland, alcohol-free, and seemingly wholesome, and their ads feature the same sort of substitute mothers and siblings found in family restaurants, only the setting is almost always the generously proportioned "country kitchen" of an upper middle-class suburban home.

FAST

Fast food restaurants originated in the 1920s, serving hurried auto tourists who did not want to waste time off the road; modern suburbanites, too, want to get in and out quickly. Large signs and well-marked driveways make it easy for speeding motorists to get off the road safely. Food must be prepared and served quickly. To save time, customers may help themselves at counters where multiple checkouts reduce waiting time. A fast food restaurant is no place for a leisurely conversation; even the faintly audible, ever upbeat background music tends to hurry you along. Similarly, convenience food must be heated up quickly and be compatible with consumer "multitasking": that is it must be easily eaten while watching television, surfing the Internet, working at a desk, or chatting on a cell phone.

FRIED

Americans love crispy fried food, but because they are often afraid to fry at home due to the vast amount of oil needed and the resultant odors, they indulge this taste at restaurants and in pre-fried takeout foods. Also, in line with the speed requirements, fried dishes can be prepared quickly and are easily carried out and eaten with fingers while multitasking. Frying also compensates for what might be termed the taste deficit inherent in reliance on many highly processed convenience foods (hence the use of all the dehydrated spices, sugars, and MSG). Packaging must be designed to keep such foods crisp while subjected to microwaving; this is no small engineering challenge. Dousing the product in cheap, extra-light olive oil also promotes a fatty "mouth feel."

FILLING

Mass-marketed meals must convey a good "perception of value"; they must fill you up yet also seem economical, "a good deal." While all cuisines rely on grains to anchor the meal, in America wheat is the filler of choice. To be both cheap and filling, dishes tend to have a lot of bread (as in the rolls) and breading (as in fried chicken). It is also easy to fill up cheaply on fried potatoes and, in a recent concession to health concerns, salad bars. Several of the ingredients in the Baltimore warehouse serve as excellent, inexpensive fillers: textured vegetable protein, modified cornstarch, and milk powder.

"FRESH"

Every cuisine has ways to certify that food is safe to eat, i.e. not "spoiled." For safety Americans look for certain bright colors, for example very green beans, very red tomatoes, very yellow pineapples, etc. (The food dye included in the Baltimore inventory comes in handy here.) Crispness, too, has meaning: fries must be firm, not mushy, lettuce brisk, not "wilted." For Americans, temperature has hygienic meaning: to be "fresh," food must be either very hot (as in fries) or very cold (as in drinks and lettuce). Tepidness is usually suspect. Energy-intensive refrigeration and air conditioning are mandatory. A sanitary atmosphere counts as well. With their shiny aluminum, tiles, and plastic, fast food restaurants try to look scrupulously clean. Kitchens are usually visible from the dining area. Strong fans eliminate objectionable frying smells. Floors and tables are scrubbed continuously. Supermarkets selling packaged convenience are always well lit, chilly, and seemingly sanitary. To be sure, much of this is for appearance only, as the often insanitary conditions of the fields, packing houses, factories, and "backstage" preparation areas that supply these sites are out of sight and mind.

FANTASY

Although the family restaurant must feel like a home from home, the fast food experience is also a form of tourism, promising escape, adventure, excitement, "a break." In today's postmodern culture at least, a food labeled "high tech" would probably not have enough fantasy value. Reflecting their ambivalence about modern urban life, consumers like nostalgic themes, especially the old West, Victorian, New England and Spanish colonial, and numerous varieties of neo-ethnic, especially Italian, Chinese, and Mexican. In urban European markets, such packaged fantasies often take on a quasi-medieval, bucolic aura: stone cottages, horse-drawn carts, filtered golden light. Suggesting a mythic world, fast food architecture and design approximate that of the Disney theme parks. Similarly, convenience foods are wrapped in the colors, scenes, and general aura of premodern "authenticity." Predictably enough, my students' television ads often entail the magical transformation of the prosaic suburban dining room/kitchen into the familiar stage sets of culinary tourism: a French café, a Tuscan villa, or a Mexican taqueria.

And yet, behind the scenes fast and convenience foods are produced by the latest, most modern technologies and arrangements. Thus in sketching out the formula, here are two more Fs that students must keep in mind (but must also keep out of *consumers'* minds).

FORDISM

In production, convenience food follows the lead of Henry Ford (1863–1947), whose assembly line manufactured cars swiftly and cheaply for the masses. Fordism is defined by a carefully organized division of labor to reduce costs and time, and a preference for automated equipment over skilled labor. Modern food workers tend to be young, unskilled, and low-paid. They are as interchangeable as the product they sell. Believing that mass production worked best if the product options were few, Ford quipped that customers could have any color – as long as it was black. Similarly, successful fast feeders hesitate to introduce new products, following McDonald's founder Ray Kroc's advice to KISS (Keep it Simple, Stupid). But just as Ford's fundamentalism soon gave way to the more segmented, multi-option marketing of General Motors, in recent years, fast food chains have begun to group themselves in "food courts" to meet consumers' diverse and fickle tastes. Likewise, convenience food marketers will offer a variety of "ethnic" versions of what trend-watcher Christopher Wolf calls "universal forms" (Belasco 2006a: 247–8). Thus "wraps" may come in Santa Fe, Thai, and spicy Mexican styles; Hormel's Marrakech Express couscous mixes offer similarly varied toppings: mango salsa, sesame ginger, Greek olive, or roasted garlic. My students catch on to this trick immediately; in their proposed line extensions they frequently substitute a red pepper for the canned pineapple, thus converting a "Hawaiian-style" burrito, burger, or pot pie into something that seems more "Latin." Fulfilling Fordist principles, the basic ingredients stay the same, but, unlike Ford's original Model T, the color is no longer just black.

FRANCHISING

Through franchising, fast food companies may expand rapidly. Most outlets are locally or regionally owned. In return for a franchise fee, the local owner is licensed to sell a certain brand and also receives management and advertising support from the central company. In effect the local owner (franchisee) supplies the capital for expansion, while the main corporation supplies the concept, aura, and ingredients. Through this unique hybrid of small and big business methods, fast food has spread across the continent – and around the globe. A similar dynamic localizes the ownership and risk of many mass-produced convenience foods, from Coke to cookies. In a sense, franchising maintains time-honored tactics and incentives of entrepreneurship while also furthering transnational consolidation and homogenization.

In addition to negotiating these complex and somewhat contradictory business challenges, Gigantic's new product development teams must also address conflicts within the organization, especially the traditional strain between engineers and marketers. Food engineers tend to think of themselves as rational, modernist scientists seeking the most elegantly functional and efficient solutions. If asked the "sleep at night" questions in the exercise, they would probably have little trouble defending what they do. They tend to dismiss consumer fears and fantasies as ill-informed, nostalgic, and subjective. An outgrowth of the humanistic aspirations of the Enlightenment, the globalizing, biochemical creed underlying the convenience cuisine has four basic principles (Belasco 2006b 111–131):

1. Everything is natural – including people, cars, DDT, Pop-Tarts. Everything is also "chemical" – including tofu, granola, and grandma's pickles. And if it contains carbon, it's "organic."
2. Nature and tradition are poor providers. If we had to rely on past ways of producing food, we would probably starve – or be much sicker. In the biochemical narrative, human history is a sorry record of plagues, pestilence, and pellagra.
3. The chemical cornucopia: only with high-tech farming and processing can we have such a wide variety of easily prepared foods year-round. Conversely, if we got all our foods seasonally and locally, our diet would be drab and boring.
4. Trust us, the experts. Why would we in the food industry want to harm our own customers? And trust the wise experts in the government, who use only "sound science" to regulate us. The system works. Only safe foods are approved.

Marketers run the food companies, however, and since their primary aim is to sell things, they are more attentive to consumer desires, however "superstitious," "emotional," and "faddish" these may seem. Thus, in the 1970s, when many consumers began to question the safety and taste of highly processed convenience foods, engineers urged their companies not to give into public "hysteria," and their food technology journals mounted fierce campaigns to "educate" the public about the safety of additives and the dangers of "natural foods." Marketers, on the other hand, saw the need to ameliorate public concerns, and they did so with a proliferation of "natural" and "organic" products – some of them genuinely healthier, many of them only superficially so. At the very minimum they understood the need to make a good impression – hence all the so-called "natural" products featuring brown packaging replete with rural iconography (barns, hand plows, whole stalks of wheat) and folksy modifiers ("country," "grandma," "valley", and "hearth") (Belasco 2006b: 185–199). A similar split occurs today over the meaning of "organic," with engineers still questioning the scientific basis of the term, while mass-marketers (including Wal-Mart) have been rolling out more and more chemical-free products, sometimes of dubious value (Fromartz 2006). More savvy about mass media than about food chemistry, my own students have no trouble pandering to popular fantasies and prejudices in their robust pitches for products such as "Hearth and Home Gourmet Stew," "Don Quixote Seven-Layer Fiesta Dip," and the rather generic but serviceable "Gourmet Delite."

In inventing their own products and campaigns, students understand well that despite the supermarket/fast food market's almost infinite array of burgers, burritos, stews, pies, and dips, most boil down to variations on a basic theme underlying all cuisines: starch and sauce. In the case of the modern market, this works out as starchy *wrapper* and *meaty* sauce. Yet despite this essential *sameness* of all meals, no food marketer is guaranteed success, for competition is fierce and results are unpredictable. While marketers may rule their companies, they do not necessarily rule the market. This may be the most difficult part of the new product development process to simulate, for students do not have to try to sell their inventions, and the ones they read about are the rare successes. To a great extent the consumer remains a mystery, as all the sophisticated techniques of market research, coordination, and salesmanship often go for naught. For example, in 2003 American manufacturers introduced over 33,000 "new" supermarket products, two-thirds of them edible – a 53 percent increase over 1993. These competed in an already crowded market, for the average supermarket had space for just 40,000 distinct items, and every shelf "slot" was already filled. Angling for rare openings on crowded shelves and in oversaturated shoppers' minds, advertisers spent billions of dollars to launch their new products – yet 50 percent of consumers interviewed in one survey could not name even one new product introduced that year.[22] No wonder then, that most new products are line extensions – the safest, most conservative form of innovation – and even most of these fail.

Further complicating our food chain analysis is that even when people do buy a product, they do not necessarily put it to the use intended by its marketers. Inside meaning changes as food moves along the chain, especially in its later steps from checkout counter to private palate. To be sure, manufacturers attempt to shape the ways foods are perceived and used – mainly through advertising, but also through promotions, placements in popular films and shows, recipes on the box, and so on. Ultimately, however, consumers can surprise you, as they use processed ingredients like canned soup, dried salad dressing mixes, Ritz crackers, and boxed gelatin desserts to construct ingenious new sauces, pastries, and casseroles. Similarly, crossing oceans in a single bound, I have adapted commercial tortillas to use as wrappers for my grandmother's potato knishes (an Eastern European stuffed pastry); in a pinch frozen filo makes excellent egg roll skins. In turn marketers may try to capitalize on such innovations through sponsored contests such as the famous Pillsbury Bake-Off, but the initial creativity usually originates at the consumer end. In the 1950s, Pillsbury required contestants to use at least a half a cup of its own flour, but to encourage novelty, it banned prepared cake mixes (Shapiro 2004: 34–40). Even the notoriously discriminating – indeed ornery – food writer M. F. K. Fisher had good things to say about home cooks who adapt, appropriate, and reconfigure corporate convenience foods. "Often they come from packages instead of canisters and barrels down [in the] cellar or in the summer pantry, but in general the boughten stuff is instinctively rejected if it tastes *too* dishonest, and once accepted by the revered ladies in the kitchens … it is treated with proper care" (Stern and Stern 1984: x).

Conversely, Laura Shapiro notes that many of the recipes deliberately concocted by food companies to hawk new products in the mid-twentieth century were soundly rejected by housewives. "Some of the dishes created by the food industry in the name of packaged-food cuisine were too peculiar for even an American to absorb, lurking as they did at the far reaches of culinary tradition without visible ties to any known combination of foods." So consumers soundly rejected company recipes for stuffing sweet potatoes with peanut butter, combining canned fruit cocktail in coleslaw, and importing frozen lemonade in salad dressing (Shapiro 2004: 57–58). "Consumer sovereignty" does work – sometimes – and must be both respected and feared.

Further complicating the marketers' job is the fact that meanings change as foods cross borders. In the process of "glocalization," transnational companies must accommodate transnational differences. In the classic work on such adaptation and appropriation, *Golden Arches East* (1997), Watson et al. examine the local uses and views of McDonald's inside five East Asian cities: Hong Kong, Beijing, Taipei, Seoul, and Tokyo. Whereas many Westerners bemoan "McDonaldization" (Ritzer 1993) as a threat to cultural diversity, local autonomy, and culinary skills, in Beijing the first McDonald's seemed a refreshing symbol of modernist sophistication and was thus welcomed as a harbinger of Chinese economic power and cultural sophistication. Later, it became a site for formal family celebrations, especially birthday parties, and thus seemed to reinforce "the harmony and solidarity of an extended family – the ideal of private life in Chinese culture" (Yan 1997: 59). A decade earlier in Taipei, McDonald's served as a vehicle by which Taiwanese could distinguish themselves *from* China, which had not yet opened itself to the chain; paradoxically, the same desire to remain independent of China led to a parallel revival of indigenous Taiwanese practices such as betel nut chewing (Wu 1997). A somewhat similar "domestication" occurred in Russia, where Muscovites "incorporated McDonald's into the more intimate and sentimental spaces of their personal lives: family celebration, cuisine and discourses about what it means to be Russian today" (Caldwell 2005: 181). Not only did McDonald's seem to support "traditional" Russian values, it also supported local farmers and entrepreneurs – a practice in many countries where franchising and domestic sourcing counter fears of globalization. Also, in many countries ingredients and flavors are adjusted for indigenous tastes and needs: for example rice dishes abound in much of Asia, in India lamb and vegetarian patties may replace beef in burgers, Finns can buy their burgers on rye buns rather than wheat, and Israelis can find McShawarmas and McKebabs (on pita bread). In all, while an outside view of McDonald's may see "the demise of the family meal," "the end of taste," and "Yankee imperialism," an inside view may see "progress," "family values," and "culinary diversity."

Sometimes such reversals can take on twists that no marketing team could devise on its own. Consider the case of SPAM, an American canned luncheon meat comprised of pork byproducts and spices. Originally popularized during the Second World War as a meat extender and substitute, it has long been considered a cheap and somewhat kitschy product in the United States. But it is also highly valued as a sign of modernity and sophistication in many parts of the Asian Pacific. For example, anthropologist Ty Matejowsky argues that even as American foodies denigrate SPAM as a symbol of the worst in American culture and cuisine, for savvy Filipinos SPAM stands for America's best aspects: abundance, luxury, freedom, and efficiency (thanks to its association with the American military, who brought it to the Philippines). And yet the dishes served up at the chic Manila fast food chain, SPAMJAM, would not be found at any American mall's food court: SPAM spaghetti, SPAM nuggets, and SPAM Caesar salad. Unlike other Pacific Asian adaptations of SPAM in sushi, tempura, and musubi (Laudan 1996: 68), these menu items have no local flavor markers, and the restaurant's décor is similarly disconnected from local surroundings. Even the American visitor "was struck by how I did not feel like I was in the Philippines." Given the rather "unassuming and blended quality" of the food and atmosphere, Filipinos can believe they are actually eating American food in a typical American shopping mall. And yet, since no such restaurant or menu can be found in America, it would be hard to call this chain an agent of Americanization. "What emerges is neither a homogenized manifestation of global culture nor a radical subversion of transnational processes but rather a simultaneous blending of Filipino and US practices, styles, preferences, and attitudes. Arguably most Filipinos would consider SPAMJAM to be preponderantly American, while most Americans would define the restaurant, especially its bill of fare, in terms almost exclusively Filipino" (Matejowsky 2007: 35–8). Paradoxically, inside meaning requires the distance of an outsider; separated by half a globe and radically different expectations, Americans and Filipinos look at the same phenomenon and find totally opposite meanings.

But consumer sovereignty and ingenuity aside, it's still SPAM, still McDonald's. Even if the inside meaning can be varied and ironic, we still need to face up to the outside meaning of such mass-marketed convenience cuisine. Nutritionally it's still meat, salt, and fat; ecologically it still uses a lot of energy and resources; and economically it's still corporate and Fordist. What then do we make of the immense and largely unexpected popularity in Japan of the Mega Mac – *four* beef patties with cheese and "special sauce" on a sesame bun? On the one hand the 2007 advertising campaign suggested an indigenous meaning to the sandwich, which required Samurai fortitude to consume. Japanese customers were so enthusiastic that stores soon ran out of supplies. But noting that it still packed 750 calories and 46 grams of fat, American observers seemed more indignant – almost embarrassed – about this apparent assault on Japanese waistlines and arteries.[23] Whose view was right? Should we take heart that consumers affix their own meanings to such mass-marketed convenience cuisine, or should that make us even more scared?

Chapter Summary

- The food industry's primary product is convenience: "We do it all for you."
- The industrial food system has lowered direct food prices for most consumers, but many of the indirect costs are hidden.
- The longer the food chain, the smaller the farmer's share of the profits and the larger the energy bill.
- If we pay less attention to food, we can pay more attention to other things.
- But something as big and vital as the food industry deserves close scrutiny and skepticism.
- Through a process of "decommodification," just a few cents' worth of simple materials are converted into a US$3.79 "meal," most of its price constituting "value added" somewhere between field and fork.
- Through commodity chain analysis we attempt to trace how food moves from field to fork, but the modern food chain is very complex and hidden.
- The current food system may be seen as an elaborate speculative scheme in which, for the sake of low prices and high fat, we are squandering our children's inheritance.
- While commodity chain analysis looks at the food system from "outside," it is also important to look at how the industry looks from "inside," i.e., the perspective of people working there.
- Fast food marketing usually follows a formula that may be best characterized as the "Eight Fs": family, fast, fried, filling, "fresh," fantasy, Fordist, franchised.
- Within food companies, marketers often disagree with engineers, especially when it comes to selling "natural" foods.
- While marketers may rule their companies, they do not necessarily rule the market, which is always uncertain, changing, and competitive.
- Consumers do not always use processed products as intended. Home cooks often adapt, appropriate, and reconfigure corporate convenience foods. And consumers abroad may "glocalize" corporate foods to suit local tastes and culture. Meanings change as foods cross borders.

5 RESPONSIBILITY: WHO PAYS FOR DINNER?

> We taste the spices of Arabia yet never feel the scorching sun which brings them forth.
>
> *Report on the East India Company* (1701)

> The cost of a thing is the amount of what I will call life which is required to be exchanged for it, immediately or in the long run.
>
> Henry David Thoreau, *Walden* (1854)

As the East India Company report implies, the global food chain was already quite extensive by 1701 – to the point where affluent English consumers could be oblivious to the costs of sweetening their tea and peppering their sausage. And such costs extended far beyond the skin burnt by the "scorching sun" of exotic foreign lands ("Arabia"). Historians of the spice trade can tally up an impressive "amount of life exchanged" – including the conquest of continents, the enslavement of nations, nasty warfare among the Eurasian powers that controlled the business, and burgeoning opportunities for pirates. Adding up the blood that was shed to stock our larders with coveted aromatics, historian Andrew Dalby concludes, "Spices are truly a dangerous taste" (Dalby 2000: 11, Pilcher 2006b: 27–33).

But do we really *want* to feel the scorching sun, to calculate the amount of life exchanged, to account for the full costs and consequences of the extraordinary banquet that most readers of this book sample every day? Perhaps not, but maybe we *should*, especially if we want to be "responsible" people. The word "responsible" derives from the Greek *sponde*, which is "to make a drink offering, to make a treaty, to pour a libation."[1] To *re-spond* is to reply to another's offering, to fulfill one's side of the bargain, to answer another's gesture, service, or gift, to participate in the mutual exchanges of commensality. From this it is a short etymological hop to being "responsible," which means meeting one's obligations to others. And to be "irresponsible" is to be untrustworthy, to cheat on a deal, to skip out on the check. Clearly few of us want to be labeled "deadbeats" or "sponges." But taking responsibility becomes vastly more complicated when attempting to count *all* the "life exchanged" in feeding us. It is one thing to pay one's restaurant bill, which usually reflects just the restaurateur's immediate costs for labor, supplies, overheads, plus a small profit margin, but it is quite another to pay one's debts to the whole food chain. To get a sense of the enormity of that bill we need to shift to an "outside" analysis of the global convenience food chain – its implications not just for our own "inside" well-being but for the welfare of others around the globe, past, present, and future.

Science fiction writer Robert Heinlein is credited with popularizing the saying, "There ain't no such thing as a free lunch" (TANSTAAFL). His context was the 1960s, when Americans were beginning to confront the environmental costs of their consumer economy.[2] But the "no free lunch" axiom dates back at least as far back as the nineteenth century, when American saloons offered complimentary food as a way to lure workers on lunch break, who either paid for their meals by buying drinks (with all the added social costs of drunkenness), or were "bounced" as "free-lunch fiends" and "loafers" (Carlin 2004). Going back much further to mythical times, the TANSTAAFL principle applies even to our primordial meals. Think about the much quoted passage from Lord Byron's epic poem, "Don Juan," which directly links "dinner" and "sinner" (1823).

> All human history attests
> That happiness for man –
> The hungry sinner –
> Since Eve ate apples,
> Much depends on dinner!

So *how* much depends on dinner? Well, quite a lot, both before that prehistoric snack and afterwards, the fateful and fatal consequences. As for the events leading up to the bite of the forbidden fruit, we might start with the six days of heavy lifting that it took God to establish the orchard. Then, in probing Eve's decision, we can cite motivations that often drive culinary experimentation – curiosity, boredom, hubris, ambition, sexual frustration, serpentine salesmanship. For the sad consequences, the downstream after-effects of Eve eating apples, Genesis suggests shame, pain, sweat, difficult childbirth, spousal abuse, the brutalization of animals, along with assorted bruised heels, dust, thorns, and thistles – the primal ecological and economic catastrophe.[3]

In the classical Greek version of TANSTAAFL, Prometheus pities shivering, starving humanity and steals fire from his less compassionate boss, Zeus. Symbolizing the primal importance of strong spices, the stolen fire is transported in a stalk of fennel. Humans learn to cook meat and to forge metal. With that technological breakthrough, they proceed to conquer the earth. But in punishment for his hubris, Prometheus is chained to a rock, where he is doomed to have his liver eaten by an eagle. Since the Promethean liver is divine and thus regenerates itself, the eagle gets to devour it every day. In a rather literalist interpretation of the story, vegetarian poet Percy Bysshe Shelley speculated that Prometheus's "vitals were devoured by the vulture of disease" (1813, quoted in Fiddes 1991: 115). Adding in the ecological costs of feeding grass and grains to animals, Shelley went on to blast the meat eater who would "destroy his constitution by devouring an acre at a meal ... The quantity of nutritious vegetable matter, consumed in fattening the carcass of an ox, would afford ten times the sustenance ... if gathered immediately from the bosom of the earth" (Belasco 2006a: 5). Such calculations were already a familiar part of vegetarian analysis a full 200 years before Frances Moore Lappé's *Diet for a Small Planet* (1971), which educated many Baby Boomers about the external costs of a meat-based diet.

The reality-based axiom of TANSTAAFL may well be universal, as it is possible to summon myths of Promethean innovation (cooking) and punishment (the ravaged liver) in many cultures.[4] For example, in some Native American versions, the people (humanity) steal fire to cook and to warm themselves; but with their new technological edge comes dire consequences, including forest fires, rain, and mosquitoes. In one Polynesian tale the mischievous superhero Maui (Prometheus's Pacific counterpart) steals cooking fire from the underworld, but as he escapes to the surface the angry flames follow him, producing the first volcano. Sociologist Claude Fischler detects more than a residue of such religious thinking in an analysis of the recent European panic over Bovine Spongiform Encephalopathy (BSE) – thought to be intensified by the thoroughly modern practice of feeding animal residues to animals: "The mad cow epidemic is perceived as punishment for some human misbehavior that caused it in the first place by attracting some sort of a sanction, the most common description of this behavior being the conversion of herbivores into carnivores or even into cannibals" (Fischler 1999: 213).

But complementing such hubristic tales of unintended consequences are dreams of a return to the innocence and ignorance of Paradise, the Golden Age *before* humans were reduced to the savage chill from which Prometheus saved them. Medieval European legends of Cockaigne envisioned a pre-Fall paradise where, according to historian Herman Pleij (2001), "Work was forbidden ... and food and drink appeared spontaneously in the form of grilled fish, roast geese, and rivers of wine. One only had to open one's mouth, and all that delicious food practically jumped inside. One could even reside in meat, fish, game, fowl, or pastry, for another feature of Cockaigne was its edible architecture." Effortless, boundless food was only one of the place's many material delights, which included eternally mild spring weather, "communal possessions, lots of holidays, no arguing or animosity, free sex with ever-willing partners, a fountain of youth, beautiful clothes for everyone, and the possibility of earning money while one slept" (3). Such fantasies took many forms, religious and secular, including intellectual daydreams about perfect utopias (Madden and Finch 2006) and actual explorations for New World sites thought to combine attributes of Eden and what Columbus called "the Spiceries," the lush Spice Islands of the Orient (Dalby 2000: 149). Some might even argue that the initial encounters with America almost fulfilled the Cockaigne dream, for here game abounded, good land seemed "free" for the taking, mostly because European diseases decimated native populations, and, all too soon, slave labor enabled whites to make money while sleeping. Every subsequent generation of new arrivals experienced the same miraculous abundance. As historian Hasia Diner argues in *Hungering for America* (2001), for immigrants the New World's streets may not have been paved with gold, but they certainly seemed full of cheap food, especially meat – the food that most enticed European peasants.

To some extent, much of the original colonial American government's goal was designed to realize this vision, as native settlements, crops, and animals were cleared out to make room for hungry European farmers, with their own seeds, weeds, and livestock. Slavery was fiercely protected for over 300 years. Territorial expansion – often at the point of the gun or bulldozer – remained official policy throughout the nineteenth and twentieth centuries, as the Federal government subsidized the replacement of Indians and Mexicans by white homesteaders, the draining of wetlands and the irrigation of drylands, the higher education of high-tech farmers, and the development of a transportation infrastructure (waterways, railroads, highways) to move agricultural products to urban markets using fossil fuels acquired through tax breaks, land seizures, and military force. Costs of this "cheap food policy" were paid by (or, in economic terms, externalized to) Indians, African slaves, Mexican and Asian farmworkers, as well as the wildlife (buffalo, birds, prairie plants) displaced by "reclamation." Favoring large-scale industrial food production that would supply the most food for the least money, federal policies hurt small-scale subsistence farmers and destroyed the same rural communities they helped to create a few generations earlier (Worster 1985; Stoll 1998; Solbrig and Solbrig 1994). The result was a lovely banquet supplied by a global food chain that could be appreciated even by 1919, when geographer J. Russell Smith marveled at the dependence of a typical Massachusetts consumer on distant sources.

> The man of today starts his breakfast with an orange from California or Florida,
> or a banana from Central America, or an apple from Oregon, Virginia, or New

York. He takes a shredded wheat biscuit made in Niagara Falls with Dakota wheat. He sugars it with the extract of Cuban cane. He puts Wisconsin butter on bread baked of Minneapolis wheat flour mixed with Illinois corn flour. He has a potato. In June it comes from Virginia, in July from New Jersey, in November from New York, Maine, or Michigan. If he indulges in meat, it is a lamb chop from a frisky little beast born on the high plains near the Rocky Mountains, and fattened in an Illinois feed lot before going up to Chicago to be inspected, slaughtered, and refrigerated. He warms and wakes himself up with a cup of coffee from Brazil (called Mocha perhaps) or tea from Ceylon or Japan, or cocoa from Ecuador or the coast of Guinea. (1919: 7)

To be sure the same story of "delocalization" could be told wherever, in pursuit of more food, one people invaded, colonized or otherwise dominated another (Pelto and Pelto 1983). Making "offers that could not be refused," to paraphrase *The Godfather's* Don Corleone, imperialists practiced cheap food policies on a global scale, yielding tasty options for Western consumers. As one British economist boasted in 1875: "The plains of North America and Russia are our cornfields, Chicago and Odessa our granaries; Canada and the Baltic our timber forests; Australia contains our sheep farms, and in South America are our herds of oxen; the Chinese grow tea for us, and our coffee, sugar, and spice plantations are all in the Indies" (Belasco 2006a: 74). The use of the royal "our" was deliberate, for in the terms of trade set by these "empires of food," the benefits flowed to the metropolitan centers in Europe, while the human costs stayed outsourced (Pilcher 2006b: 71–78). The East India Company's claim about its customers not feeling the "scorching sun" pretty much acknowledged as much.

Where advocates of such trade saw Progress, anti-imperialists detected the "Big Grab" and the "Bandit Plan" of "colonize–destroy–move on" (Belasco 2006a: 74). Deploring in 1924 the systematic "plunder" by which the West fed itself, geneticist Edward East predicted that the Victorians' "Belshazzar's Feast" would soon be over, as soils were becoming depleted, new colonies were becoming hard to find, and the already colonized were rebelling (East 1924: 9). East was alluding to the Book of Daniel story in which Babylonian King Belshazzar wined and dined his legions using sacred vessels sacked from the Jewish Temple in Jerusalem. During the feast the ominous "writing on the wall" appeared in the banquet hall: *Mene mene tekel upharsin.* Frightened Belshazzar summoned his Hebrew advisor Daniel, who in a rather freewheeling interpretation, translated the divine graffiti as "Thou art weighed in the balance and art found wanting." Soon after the king was murdered and replaced by Darius the Mede, who ordered more respect for Daniel's people. The story is full of historical flaws – scholars dispute whether there was in fact a Belshazzar or a Darius the Mede – but the larger message about a divine accounting holds considerable power, for it suggests that excess is unsustainable and will be avenged. No wonder, then, that those who attempt to warn us against irresponsible consumption often speak of "the writing on the wall" – or employ other prophetic language such as "mankind at the crossroads," "wake-up call," "reaping a bitter harvest," and "so shall you reap."

HEALTH COSTS: FOOD-BORNE ILLNESS

Where to begin such an accounting? Long ago journalist Upton Sinclair discovered that consumers are most concerned about food issues that affect their own personal health. While *The Jungle* (1906) was intended as an exposé of harsh working conditions in the slaughterhouses, his readers were most outraged by the threats to their own health posed by insanitary meat production. Personal disgust, not social compassion drove the campaign for food industry regulation. "I aimed for their hearts," Sinclair later sighed, "but hit their stomachs." A similar fate awaited Eric Schlosser's *Fast Food Nation* (2001), which is largely a description of fast food business practices, including once again its infamous slaughterhouse working conditions, yet which is most well known for its single, stomach-churning chapter on *E. coli*, "What's in the Meat?" But as both Sinclair and Schlosser demonstrated, the personal could not be easily disentangled from the political. Intimate threats such as food poisoning are directly linked to the length and complexity of the food chain, so even if we start with our own stomachs, the local quickly becomes global.

To return to Paul Rozin's formulation (page 2), eating sustains us – it is "fundamental" – but it also very "frightening," for it may make us sick, maybe tomorrow or maybe in thirty years. The former, immediate dangers may be labeled "acute," the latter, more distant dangers, "chronic." Both forms of diet-related illness may be the result of modern lifestyles and food industry practices.

If today's dinner makes us sick tomorrow, it's usually what we call "food poisoning," or more precisely "food-borne illness." In 2005 almost 2 million people worldwide died of diarrheal diseases, most of them food-related. The US Centers for Disease Control (CDC) estimate 76 million American cases of food-borne diseases a year, resulting in 325,000 hospitalizations and 5,000 deaths. While food-borne microbes have been killing humans for millennia – think of the millions slain by cholera alone – today's carnage in the more modernized nations results from newly emerging variants of *Salmonella* serotype Enteritidis (*SE*), *Escherichia coli* serotype O157:H7 (*E. coli*), *Campylobacter jejuni,* and *Listeria monocytogenes* (*Lm*) that seem to thrive in a globalized food chain. In 2005 the World Health Organization reported a 30 percent annual increase in industrialized countries. "Food contamination creates an enormous social and economic burden on communities and their health systems," the WHO continued. "In the USA, diseases caused by the major pathogens alone are estimated to cost up to US$35 billion annually (1997) in medical costs and lost productivity."[5]

Such numbers are of course quite soft and variable. Most cases are not reported anyway, as people dismiss their illness as "24-hour flu." And there is no single agreed-upon standard to measure the full bill for an outbreak – despite pernicious efforts by neo-liberal administrations to quantify the value of a human life as a way to weaken, or at least constrain, environmental and consumer safety regulation. According to such "cost-benefit analysis" the value of lives saved has to be "worth" the costs of prevention. Value, indeed. Given the inherent subjectivity of such calculations, nutritionist Marion Nestle notes a very wide range in United States estimates of the social costs of food-borne illness: from US$4.8 billion to US$23 billion in 1989, and from US$13 billion in 1996 to US$37 billion in 1997. "Whatever the correct figure may be, it surely underestimates the costs to the victims in pain and inconvenience; to taxpayers in medical treatment for the indigent, higher health insurance premiums, public health surveillance systems, and investigations of outbreaks (estimated at US$200,000 each); and to the food industry in plant closings, cleanup, and recalls as well as in legal fees, claim settlements, and higher insurance premiums" (Nestle 2003: 39). The somewhat arbitrary lines drawn by public health authorities can be seen in one 2000 American report, which put the costs of just five major bacterial pathogens at US$6.9 billion. The USDA's Economic Research Service calculations included "medical costs, productivity losses from missed work, and an estimate of the value of premature death that takes into account the age distribution of those taken ill. The estimate excludes travel costs in obtaining medical care, lost leisure time, and so forth."[6] One does wonder about the "so forth."

On the other hand, British calculations of the costs of food-borne diseases did seem to include some of the "so forth," at least to the extent of "pain, grief, and suffering."[7] But how *does* one measure "grief and suffering," or the lost social contributions of an individual who, had she not been killed by *E. coli* in a burger at age six, might have grown up to be a great teacher, scientist, or prime minister? In a critique of environmental cost-benefit analysis, Heinzerling and Ackerman conclude, "Cost-benefit analysis cannot overcome its fatal flaw: it is completely reliant on the impossible attempt to price the priceless values of life, health, nature, and the future" (Heinzerling and Ackerman 2002: 33).

While it may be impossible to calculate full future losses, it is hard enough to quantify *present* dangers. Accurate statistics are difficult to achieve because, as Nestle says, "Food safety is political" (1–25). The food business is the world's largest industry, and thanks to the "revolving door," many top regulatory officials come from or are headed to the companies they regulate. Moreover, much as the food companies are torn between the differing desires of marketers and engineers – not to mention by the consumer's conflicting demands (see Chapter 4) – governments are fragmented by different constituencies, agendas, and paradigms (Belasco 2006b: 132–153; Barling 2004; Hoffmann and Taylor 2005; Lien and Nerlich 2005). The same governments that regulate food safety – and tally the body count when regulation fails – also promote agricultural production and commerce, both domestic and export. Nothing more discourages foreign demand for one's chickens than reports of salmonella, or worse, avian flu. Governments also promote and even subsidize the local tourist industry whose success requires at least the illusion that travelers will not be poisoned by their holiday meals. As the Food and Agriculture Organization notes, such self-interest is a disincentive to report the full extent of microbial threats.[8] (The US CDC estimates that somewhere between 20 and 50 percent of international travelers – 10 million victims – will come down with "travelers' diarrhea" each year.[9]) And sometimes regulation is divided between different agencies with different mandates. "Today," Nestle observes, "an inventory of federal food safety activities reveals a system breathtaking in its irrationality: thirty-five separate laws administered by twelve agencies housed in six cabinet-level departments" (55). The resulting delegation of responsibility is worthy of an absurdist play – or of Charles Dickens's 1857 description in *Little Dorrit* of the government bureaucracy from hell: "Whatever was required to be done, the Circumlocution Office was beforehand with all the public departments in the art of perceiving HOW NOT TO DO IT."[10] For example the USDA oversees pizza with meat toppings, the FDA cheese pizza; USDA regulates open-face meat and poultry sandwiches, FDA the closed-face versions (Nestle 2004: 55–57). Complicating the regulatory mess is the divided oversight among legislative bodies, where dozens of committees and, in the case of the European Union, dozens of national parliaments, all angle to represent local interests – and to keep competing interests from, in Dickens's words, "doing it."

As political bodies, governments are also mindful of the modern consumer's desire for food that is both cheap and safe – a major contradiction especially when it comes to producing and distributing animal foods, which are by their nature highly perishable (Nestle 2004: 62–138). Just as ancient regimes fell when bread prices rose, modern politicians worry about rising meat prices. How much are consumers willing to pay for antibiotic-free animals that are not overcrowded in industrial farms and feedlots? Organic meat, egg, and dairy production may reduce the microbial threat, but its higher costs are voluntarily borne, not dictated throughout society. Locally produced food may be safer because it does not travel halfway around the world picking up hitchhiking bugs at the numerous transfer points en route. Also, local producers who must directly face their customers are more easily held accountable for food quality than are unseen suppliers in distant countries. But cheese or tomatoes at a farmer's market will always be more expensive than Wal-Mart's industrial version, and governments would certainly hesitate to impose the higher costs of local food on *everyone*. And how much are we ready to pay to improve training and working conditions in the fields, animal factories, and processing plants? Simple reforms such as reducing line speed, providing more sanitary facilities, and educating workers in basic sanitation greatly reduce the potential for contamination. In grocery stores and restaurants higher wages, profit sharing, more breaks, paid sick leave, and stronger unions to enforce all of these benefits have been shown to improve morale and sanitation in the overstressed meat and deli departments, but these do come at a price.

And how much more are we willing to pay for more government supervision at every stage of the food chain? Judging by the general aversion to taxes, not very much – especially when the worst risks are borne by others, particularly the poor and disenfranchised. After all, while the FAO estimates that a third of the population in industrial populations may suffer from food-borne illness every year, "the problem is likely to be even more widespread in developing countries. The poor are the most susceptible to ill health. Food and waterborne diarrheal diseases, for example, are leading causes of illness and death in less developed countries, killing an estimated 2.1 million people annually, most of whom are children."[11] A somewhat similar profile holds in the richer nations: those likely to suffer the most are young children, the elderly, and the already ill. And among these demographics, the poor receive the worst healthcare and are thus most vulnerable. Particularly worrisome but not surprising, then, are reports of food-borne outbreaks in government-subsidized school lunch programs – the last nutritional resort for many poor children. And when in 1999 a beef processor that supplied almost half of the national school lunch program's ground beef filed a suit against the USDA's new salmonella-testing requirements, a federal appeals court sided with the processor; lacking allies in Congress and industry, the USDA decided not to appeal (Nestle 2004: 104–107). Chalk another one up for HOW NOT TO DO IT.

Considering all these added costs and political challenges, it should not be surprising that when it comes to patrolling food, industry and government websites shove the lone consumer to the frontline of defense against microbes. From the perspective of www.foodsafety.gov, if everyone simply refrigerated and defrosted their food properly, washed it thoroughly in clean running water, took care to use separate cutting boards and knives for meat, and then overcooked it afterwards (using an accurate food thermometer), there would be no microbial safety problem. To this might be added a few other simple precautions, like having your chuck ground and wrapped in front of you at the meat counter, packing it in a cooler (with handy freezer packs), and then speeding home before it starts to decay. And if you are eating out, Alaska's Food Safety and Sanitation program has a few simple tips: inspect the servers for cleanliness (making especially sure that their fingernails are clean), scrutinize all sides of the dishes and utensils, take a glance at the condition of the floor, make sure the salad bar ingredients "smell fresh," "try to get a glimpse of the person preparing your food," insist that the food is served either very cold or very hot (presumably with that handy food thermometer), and leave immediately if you spot any bugs.[12] In other words, *caveat emptor* (Fox 1997).

HEALTH COSTS: FATNESS

If it is hard to identify and take responsibility for acute "bellyaches" that would have seemed quite familiar to Upton Sinclair's readers a hundred years ago, it is much tougher calculating and confronting the costs of the newer, chronic "diseases of affluence" – i.e., the modern illnesses that may not kill you tomorrow but rather thirty years from now: heart disease, diabetes, cancer. While food-borne outbreaks may be tracked back to particular factories and even, with new traceability requirements, to particular animals, it is impossible to attribute an individual case of colon cancer to a certain hamburger, or even a lot of hamburgers, consumed decades earlier. Producer liability – difficult enough to prove with salmonella – becomes nearly impossible to demonstrate with heart attacks or strokes. And yet, epidemiological statistics indicate that how and what we eat may be threatening our long-term health, and the full costs to us all may be enormous, perhaps even catastrophic.

While fatness has long been a focus of medical and cultural concern (Stearns 1997, Schwartz 1986), alarming recent trends have promoted it to the status of an "epidemic." According to the Centers for Disease Control, the percentage of American adults who were considered obese almost tripled between 1960 and 2000 (from 11 percent to 33 percent). During the 1990s alone the percentage of obese adults increased by almost half, from 23 percent to 33 percent; during that same period the percentage of adults considered "overweight" increased from 56 percent to 65 percent (Brownell 2004: 41; Squires 2002: A18). And the bill for all this? In one widely publicized report, the CDC estimated that in 2000 almost as many Americans would die from poor eating habits and physical inactivity (400,000 – up 33 percent since 1990) as from smoking (435,000, up just 9 percent from 1990).[13] In the process of dying, they would, of course, consume a lot of healthcare services. In 2001 the US Surgeon General estimated the direct and indirect costs of fatness at US$117 billion a year (Dalton 2004: 201). Another study by health economists attributes about 9 percent of America's trillion dollar healthcare bill to the costs of treating weight-related diseases; of this half is paid by Medicare and Medicaid, both of which are in shaky condition and not up to the job of financing the healthcare of aging Baby Boomers (Finkelstein et al. 2003).

And considering the declining fitness of the Boomers' children, the more distant future looks even worse. During the 1990s, according to the CDC, fatness among children aged six to eleven doubled (to 13 percent), and tripled among adolescents (to 14 percent) (Dietz 2005: 2). If anything these numbers may have been too conservative, with some experts calculating that 25–30 percent of American children were either overweight or *at risk* of becoming so (Dalton 2004: 16). Such statistics are particularly troublesome because fat teenagers almost always become fat adults. And with more fatness comes more chronic disease, particularly hypertension, some forms of cancer, and Type-2 diabetes, "an illness associated with cardiovascular disease, stroke, limb amputations, kidney failure, and blindness." Once called "adult-onset diabetes," the Type-2 variety is no longer waiting for adulthood, with the American Diabetes Association reporting that it may now account for almost half of the new diabetes cases among children. Combining these trends, some studies suggest that "One in three healthy children born will develop diabetes unless they start eating less and increasing their physical activity." The prognosis is worse for minority children, with nearly half of black and Hispanic children likely to develop diabetes during their lifetimes. This higher incidence reflects the fact that the people most vulnerable to fat-related diseases are poor minorities, especially women. According to the CDC, "Women of lower socioeconomic status ... are approximately 50 percent more likely to be obese that those of higher socioeconomic status." Over 80 percent of non-Hispanic women of color and 75 percent of Mexican-American women were either overweight or obese; for non-Hispanic white women the figure was 58 percent.[14] Given that by 2050, one in two Americans are likely to be a racial or ethnic minority, such statistics are ominous indeed (Dietz 2005 1–2).

While many commentators use these numbers to stigmatize Americans as being exceptionally lazy, gluttonous, hedonistic, and otherwise morally flabby, the trend is global. According to the World Health Organization, in 2003 over a billion adults were overweight, 300 million of them obese, with similarly alarming rates of increase in many parts of the world. More than half the adults in the United Kingdom, Spain, Australia, Brazil, Mexico, Denmark, Italy, and Russia were overweight. Despite self-perceptions of virtue, 40 percent of French adults were overweight in 2006, with rates running over 50 percent in depressed northern areas. Obesity rates among French children were increasing by 16 percent a year, and the French died of obesity-related diseases at almost the same rate as Americans. Noting a tripling of British obesity in 20 years (to about 20 percent of adults), the UK's National Health Service estimated obesity-related healthcare costs at £500 million, with total costs to the economy of at least £3 billion. Obesity rates also approach 20 percent in some Chinese cities; in Thailand child obesity rates soared from 12 to 15 percent in just two years. Thanks perhaps to the successful "glocalization" of fast food in these areas (see Chapter 4), urban children are become fatter worldwide, with the same vulnerability to diabetes, hypertension, cancer and other weight-related illnesses.[15]

What makes these trends so troubling is that they appear to punish us for doing what we humans are *supposed* to be doing: evolving from a state of chronic hunger and hard labor – the universal experience for most of our history – to an almost utopian, Cockaigne-like state of satiety and ease. Epidemiologist Adam Drewnowski argues that humans are essentially programmed to love sugar and fat, as an innate preference for sweetness (the "sweet tooth") helps to direct infants toward vital sources of nutrients and calories, while our "fat tooth" equips us to seek out the most concentrated source of energy (Drewnowski 1999: 197). According to the "thrifty gene" theory, millions of years of perpetual scarcity favored humans who could store fat during the rare periods of abundant calories; when scarcity returned, as it did often, the extra fat kept our ancestors alive long enough to pass on their "thrifty genes"(Critser 2003: 129–130). But now, with so many calories consistently available, the fat stays on.

And in another cruel trick, our utilitarian propensity to seek convenience – the "law of least action," the driver of Progress – now works against us, as we have fewer opportunities to work off the calories. The evolutionary dilemma is perhaps most visible among those who have transitioned most quickly from states of subsistence to quick 'n' easy abundance: e.g., Alaskan natives, Samoans, Australian Aborigines, and Bedouins. Soon after the arrival of profitable casinos, 7-Elevens, and fast food, almost half of Arizona's Pima Indians developed diabetes – the world's highest rate – in stark contrast to their leaner, tougher cousins across the border in rural Mexico (Brownell 2004: 22). Similarly a comparison of Mayans in Guatemala and in the US finds that the latter have experienced "the greatest one-generation gains in height ever," with equally huge weight gains (Critser 2003: 130).

The cultural contradictions are almost as cruel, for the fatness epidemic seems to reverse many centuries of hopes and dreams. For much of history fatness had been rightfully identified with prosperity, power, and privilege – associations that still hold in very poor societies where only a few have access to surplus. Reflecting that historic experience of scarcity, fat is still considered "sweet" in many rural areas of the Third World, and through ritual feasting the poor attempt to plump each other up. Indeed, to be thin in rural Jamaica is to be considered "mean or stingy," a person not nurturing or caring (Sobo 1997; Kulick and Meneley 2005). In a sense, since the Enlightenment, it has been the goal of democratic reform to fatten *everyone* up – i.e., to provide more food for more people, especially meat (the nutrition transition), more postindustrial "services" (restaurants, convenience stores, home-delivered pizza), and less drudgery for cooks. As we have seen, the defenders of convenience food have been very happy to claim this progressive role, but now this same Progress is our nemesis – even to the extent of shortening our lives. Contradicting the long-held expectation of greater longevity, obesity researchers now predict that, thanks to modern food's fatal mix of fat and convenience, future generations might have shorter lives. "Within fifty years, if the trend is not reversed, obesity will cut the average life span by at least two to five years, which would exceed the effects of all cancers ... That could overtake all gains from healthier lifestyles and medical advances and cause longevity to plateau or perhaps decline."[16] Given such recent assessments, it is not surprising that hope for a better future has declined sharply since the onset of the much-awaited New Millennium (Belasco 2006a: 257–261).

Americans may have especially good reasons to feel betrayed by Progress, for abundant food, particularly meat, has been a mainstay of the national identity since colonial times. As suggested earlier, federal farm policy has been enormously successful in subsidizing high-tech food production and distribution. A deliberate byproduct of the government's "cheap food policy," America's perennial glut of grain, sugar, and milk enables – indeed encourages – food marketers to convert that surplus into a rich array of high-calorie drinks, burgers, and snacks. Meanwhile US foreign policy focuses hard on securing supplies of cheap petroleum, which allows almost all its citizens drive to and through McDonald's; the right *not* to walk is an American entitlement. And for decades the US government pushed dietary advice that privileged meat and dairy products; of the highly influential Basic Four Food Groups, two consisted of animal foods – a very convenient boon to the livestock industry, and to the grain farmers who supplied them. Moderation, portion control, self-denial – all are values foreign to American restaurants and supermarkets that even today, amidst the fatness "epidemic," continue to flaunt cornucopian excess.

Furthering the American letdown is the fact that, of all societies, US society may be the most "diet-conscious," as Americans spend somewhere between US$40 and US$100 billion a year on weight-control products, books, and services. Such statistics are notoriously inexact, yet they do tend to be repeated over and over in articles that alternately applaud and deplore this apparent "obsession" with calorie control. Indeed the diet industry marches in almost perfect sync with some very basic American faiths and notions:

1. *Faith in individual perfectability*: American do believe that you *can* make yourself over, start anew, overcome obstacles, defy the odds, have a second (and third) chance, make a fresh start, especially after New Year's Day, when enrollments in gyms and weight-loss programs traditionally skyrocket.

Box 5.1. Toward Mindful Eating

The roots of the obesity epidemic are suggested in the title of marketing psychologist Brian Wansink's *Mindless Eating, Why We Eat More Than We Think* (2006). When food is plentiful, attractive, and easily accessible, Wansink's many experiments show, people will eat it more of it, almost automatically, without thought. Conversely, when people are mindful of what they are eating, they eat less. As a step toward more consciousness, try the following exercise: For seven days, keep a record of all eating occasions, including "snacks." In particular, write down, in a chart:

1. When you ate it and how long it took to eat it.
2. The number of people you ate with (people you actually know).
3. Where you ate it.
4. Who prepared it.
5. The cost of your portion of this meal.
6. The geographical source of the #1 ingredient (i.e., Iowa, Chile, Florida, etc. If you don't know, say "Don't know").
7. The predominant taste sensations.
8. The nutritional composition of what you ate, including these numbers, which may be derived using the USDA's online Nutrient Data Laboratory.[23]
   — Total weight in grams. (Note that USDA does this by average portion size, which is often a lot less than what people actually eat.)
   — Energy (kcal).
   — Protein (grams).
   — Total lipid (fat) (grams).
   — Saturated fatty acids (grams).
   — Cholesterol (mg).
9. Looking back at the seven days, please calculate:
   — Your average daily calorific intake (total kilocalories divided by 7).
   — The percentage of total kilocalories that were derived from fat. (To do this, multiply your number of grams of total lipid times 9, then divide this number by your total kilocalories.)
   — The percentage of total kilocalories consumed away from home.
10. Finally, analyze the significance of the week's food consumption:
    — What surprises you most about what and how you ate over those seven days?
    — How did keeping a food diary affect your food consumption?
    — Complete this sentence: "If we are what we eat, then I am ..."

2. *Faith in individual willpower*: Ask an American this question: "Is it true that anyone can lose weight if s/he wants to?" The answers will be almost universally affirmative, even among students well schooled in the environmental and biological determinants of fatness. Following positive thinkers such as Benjamin Franklin, Horatio Alger, and Norman Vincent Peale, Americans believe that if you *want* to do it, you *can* do it. Conversely, if you fail, it's because you didn't try hard enough.

3. *The ability to control nature*: A nation that straightened the Mississippi, made the deserts bloom, and leveled whole mountains can surely control its own waistline. We can defy the biological determinism of thrifty genes, fat and sweet teeth, and metabolic set points, as well as the naturally fattening processes of pregnancy, childbirth, and aging.

4. *The priority of youth*: Unlike many Old World cultures, Americans prize youthfulness, which is associated with thinness.

5. *A mechanistic view of the body*: The body is not an organism but a machine, whose inputs can be closely calculated (via calorie counting) and whose parts can be adjusted (via "spot" exercises).

6. *The Protestant ethic*: Calvinistic self-denial will be rewarded. No pain, no gain.

7. *Faith in consumer capitalism*: Since almost all diets fail, there is considerable repeat business. The diet industry is a classic case of capitalistic enterprise built around perpetual obsolescence (the constant flow of "new and improved" products).

As if to reinforce – indeed compel – compliance with these beliefs, a mass-mediated culture offers up impossibly thin body images in advertising, film, and television. On the other hand, people considered obese are socially stigmatized and materially punished. Surveys routinely find that Americans value thinness above all other personal or social goals and would do almost anything – even to the point of giving up five years of life – to lose weight.[17] Pushed and pulled by these powerful incentives, many children start "dieting" in elementary school. Eating disorders are endemic, if not epidemic. Of these, anorexia nervosa may be the most dire, but bulimia and binge eating may be more common – in part because they almost make "sense" in a schizophrenic culture that emphasizes both extreme self-indulgence and self-punishment. But it would be fallacious to isolate American culture. Just as fatness is spreading across the globe, so too is the obsession with thinness. Even in desperately poor countries of the Sahel, where women are deliberately fattened up to make them more desirable, counter-images of impossibly thin Westernized beauty are beginning to take hold among urban youth. "Some girls have asked me whether they should get fat or stay thin," a 19-year-old Mauritanian male observes. "I tell them if you want to find a man, a European or a Mauritanian, stay thin, it's better for you."[18] Will food disorders follow soon after?

And yet, all this angst, vigilance, and self-flagellation are of little avail, as the epidemiological news seems to get worse every year. Noting the striking consistency of the dreary obesity numbers cited to compel public attention, some skeptics have questioned the statistics themselves. How solid *are* they? Is it really *that* bad? And why so *sudden* a surge in fatness? After all fast food, cars, and sedentary lifestyles were the Western norm for many decades before the statistical uptick of the 1990s. Why now? Might something else be going on? Is the increase in fatness really an "epidemic" or is it perhaps the focus of a "moral panic," in which deeper economic, political, and cultural anxieties are being projected on the fat? There *are* a lot of crises to worry about nowadays, including climate change, terrorism, a possible avian flu pandemic, worldwide migration, economic uncertainties, over thirty ongoing wars, the decline of Western hegemony, and so on. Might the focus on fatness be a tangible, but perhaps misplaced *embodiment* of our fears and a convenient place to focus our need to assert some control over our destiny? And more particularly, control over women, who are more likely to be worried about their weight? As some feminists have been arguing for decades, the war on fatness has long been used as an instrument to keep women in line – and quite successfully so (e.g., Sobal and Maurer 1999a and 1990b; Newman 1995; Gard and Wright 2005; Campos 2004; Orbach 2006).

Moreover, in the hurry to claim a "crisis," might there be some exaggeration of the threat, especially in the frequent conflation of "overweight" and "obese." While few doubt the problems of extreme obesity, many more of us may just be heavy, and is that necessarily harmful? The rush to condemn the majority of us as "fat" and "at risk" reminds some critics of the infamous insurance company "ideal weight" charts of the 1920s that deemed just about every adult to be overweight and thus doomed to an early death (Schwartz 1986: 156). Even so, fatness notwithstanding, humans have been living longer all over the world.

But even if the epidemic is real – the alarming figures about Type-2 diabetes are hard to dispute – the cure is by no means clear. Perhaps the mounting hysteria results from our uncertainty about who will pay for it. The economic stakes could be enormous, with skyrocketing health insurance costs threatening to bankrupt corporations and governments alike. With such a huge bill looming, it is tempting to shift responsibility. Is fatness the fault and thus the liability of the fat, or do we ask everyone to share the costs? Answering this multi-billion (perhaps trillion) dollar question requires that we look for the real causes of fatness and obesity. Explanations tend to group themselves in three concentric circles of ever-widening responsibility.

1. *Individuals.* The narrowest – and perhaps most popular – is that the fat themselves are responsible for their own overeating and inactivity. The solution: Stop eating and move your butt. And if you don't, suffer! Or pay your *own* bills. And if you can't, then society will finance your bills with taxes on fat in food – an indirect way of getting you to pay. Conversely, by steering clear of fat-laden foods and exercising more, the virtuously thin might get a break in their grocery and insurance bills.

2. *Environment.* A considerably more comprehensive circle of blame targets a pervasive "toxic food environment" that leads us down the treacherous path of overeating: for example, junk food advertising and in-school promotions directed at children, "supersizing" of portions, rushed, stressful lives, loss of cooking skills, decline of family meals, etc. And on the inactivity side, an equally toxic built environment promotes automobility and discourages physical exercise. For solutions, this perspective looks largely to government reforms that would simultaneously restrain marketing excesses and redesign the landscape. Those concerned about the apparent decline of family dining – often cited as a contributing factor – might also call for more legislation (dating from the early twentieth century, the Progressive Era) to enhance family dining – e.g., shorter work hours, more vacations, family leave, cooking classes in schools, and so on (Brownell and Horgen 2004; Dixon and Broom 2007; Critser 2003).

    In more radical versions of this critique (also dating back to Progressives like Upton Sinclair), state-supported capitalism is itself the culprit, as it benefits from overeating. Enabled by the considerable public subsidies noted earlier, the food industry does exactly what it is supposed to do: make money. Fat-promoting foods are profitable, and so are the byproducts – the hundreds of billions spent on medical care. The ultimate environmental solution: Nationalize the food industry. As the old countercultural slogan went, "Food for people, not for profit."

3. *Stratification.* Noting the race, class, and gender parameters of the epidemic – especially the fact that poor minority women suffer the most – an even more subversive analysis blames deeply seated patterns of discrimination and inequality. Obesity is a symptom of poverty, racism, and sexism. To be sure, there may be individuals of all strata who are genetically disposed to be obese – and they can be treated within the existing system – but obesity is *socially constructed* as a *crisis* mainly because it is increasing disproportionately among those least able to pay for its effects. With more economic, social, and political power, the reasoning goes, these disenfranchised groups will have access to better food, better healthcare, and

better environments. Going beyond the top-down, nationalizing propensities of the environmentalist view, this perspective comes close to advocating radical social change from below (Fraser 1997; Nasser 1997; Germov and Williams 1999; Sobal and Maurer 1999a, 1999b; Kulick and Meneley 2005; Coveney 2006).

Given the potentially high economic costs of #2 and the even greater social dislocations implied by #3, no wonder that popular discourse attempts to stay at the level of #1, where the fat pay for their own "mistakes" and the rest of us are free to go for seconds at the buffet.

CONFRONTING THE EXTERNALITIES

But if we're fortunate enough not to get sick from eating, does that let us off the responsibility hook? Not if we think about the *external* costs of our banquet. Focusing on the *internal* food-related illnesses, whether acute or chronic, implies that the consumer does somehow "pay" a stiff price for eating the wrong things. This is the Genesis story, which punishes Adam and Eve for their culinary sins. But what about cases where the consumer gets along just fine, while *others* subsidize the banquet with their own pain? That is the story of Prometheus. He suffers so humans may roast their meat. Specifically, his ravaged liver becomes an *external* cost of our expanded dining options.

Consider three externalities of the Nutrition Transition to a diet rich in animal products and other luxuries: costs to animals, to workers, and to the planet itself.

What do we owe the billions of breathing creatures who provide our milk and cheese, eggs, meat, feathers, hides, and wool? And how much more are we willing to pay to minimize their suffering and sacrifice? Given the importance of animal foods in the narrative of progress, the general direction of history has been to make them cheaper and easier to consume, and with that comes an equally long and compelling narrative of vegetarian protest and moral cost-accounting (Fiddes 1991; Spencer 1995; Walters and Portmess 1999; Maurer 2002).

In many ways the animal industry represents the leading edge of industrial mass production (Giedion 1969; Horowitz 2006). Fordism should be called Swiftism after the ruthlessly efficient animal disassembly line that predated the automotive version. Following spices, sugar, and flour, animals may have been among the earliest components of the modern diet to be "distanced" from consumers, as their tending, slaughter, and processing were rendered invisible by railroads and steamships, acute division of labor, refrigeration, power saws, nitrites, and cellophane. "The greater the degree of mechanization," historian of technology Siegfried Giedion writes, "the further does contact with death become banished from life" (242). Conversely, closing that gap seems essential to paying the full costs of animal foods. But if, as William Cronon writes, the Chicago meat-packers thrived on "forgetfulness," (1991: 256), do we really want to remember how the burger got to our bun? (Ozeki 1999; Lovenheim 2002).

Anthropologists document that many cultures thank the animal personally before eating her; some even elevate their meat sources to the status of mythic heroes (Fiddes 1991). In the modern world, however, we often resent the people who try to remind us of the bloody facts of life. Such at least has been the result of an experiment I have been conducting with my students over the last twenty years (see Box 5.2). Specifically, I ask each student to read a highly inflammatory quotation to at least five people outside of the university and record their reactions. The passage comes from *The Penitent*, a novel by Nobel laureate Isaac Bashevis Singer, who was a vegetarian. Strong stuff, made doubly so by the Nazi reference, which is a red flag in polite discourse – though not entirely inappropriate here, as Nazis did ship their human victims in "cattle cars" to extermination camps that operated with almost the same dispassionate, industrial efficiency as modern slaughterhouses (Hilberg 1961). Moreover, many of the eugenic principles used to rationalize the systematic destruction of European Jews, Gypsies, homosexuals, and other "defective" peoples were adapted from the selective breeding practices of the modern animal industry (Kevles 1985). Indeed, for some animal rights advocates, the only significant difference is semantic: the Nazis *concentrated* their victims, while the meat industry *confines* theirs (Mason and Singer 1990).

But since many respondents are so offended by any equation of human and animal holocausts that they focus their outrage on Singer rather than the pig, I have dropped that sentence in some questionnaires. Even without the Nazi hyperbole, however, most respondents vehemently reject Singer's concern about animal welfare or rights. Their reactions group themselves into several categories of rationalization, each of which suggests that people trying to prevent cows from becoming burgers have a very tough challenge. This may be why so many vegetarian activists feel they need to be obnoxious; how else to prod the complacent public out of the protective cocoon of self-serving conventional wisdom?

What is perhaps most remarkable in these defenses of meat eating is that relatively few respondents cite taste or identity for their primary rationale. "I eat meat because I like it" does not seem a sufficient counter to Singer's savage critique. Nutrition *is* sometimes cited in the defenses, although "healthy" and "good for you" are considered questionable assets in food marketing. Many decades of government- and industry-supported dietary propaganda have left the (debatable) impression that animal foods are the best, indeed *only* good source of protein. Some mistakenly

---

Box 5.2. The Meat Religion

The purpose of this exercise is to help us understand why most people seem to be committed to a meat-centered diet and why reformers face a steep uphill battle in their attempts to convince us of the moral, ecological, and health benefits of a more vegetarian diet. In this exercise you need to find FIVE people from a variety of backgrounds (especially in age, gender, class). Record and analyze their answers to these difficult questions:

1. Are you a vegetarian? If so, when did you become one and why? (Vegetarians skip questions 2 and 3.)
2. If you do eat meat, please fill in the blanks: I eat meat because _____. I could not be a vegetarian because _____.
3. If you do eat meat, do you eat the same amount and type of meat as you did when you were growing up? Explain why you've changed or haven't changed.
4. How have you reacted to reports about the negative health effects of eating meat?
5. How do you react to the following statement by a character in *The Penitent*, a novel by Isaac Bashevis Singer (Nobel laureate for literature):

   "I watched someone at the next table working away at his plate of ham with eggs. I had long since come to the conclusion that man's treatment of God's creatures makes mockery of all his ideals and the whole alleged humanism. In order for this overstuffed individual to enjoy his ham, a living creature had to be raised, dragged to its death, tortured, scalded in hot water. The man didn't give a second's thought to the fact that the pig was made of the same stuff as he and that it had to pay with suffering and death so that he could taste its flesh. I've more than once thought that when it comes to animals, every man is a Nazi." (1983: 27)

   Do you (a) Agree totally, (b) Agree somewhat, or (c) Disagree totally? Please explain.
6. Read the chapters on meat production in Eric Schlosser's *Fast Food Nation* and then write one paragraph (250 words) to summarize his most disturbing points. Then read that paragraph to your respondents and ask them: "Are you (a) Bothered enough to consider rethinking your diet, (b) Somewhat bothered, but not enough to change your diet, or (c) Not bothered at all? Please explain."

Analysis. What do the above responses signify about current attitudes toward meat? How do your responses compare to those summarized on page 99? What would it take to motivate people to eat less meat?

---

believe that the alternative is just "vegetables" of the leafy green variety, rather than the more varied diet of grains, nuts, legumes, eggs, and dairy products consumed by most vegetarians. But the debate with Singer's quote is generally *not* fought on these personal grounds. Instead of citing the taste and nutrition reasons for eating meat (and killing animals), most respondents seem compelled to take the debate to a seemingly higher level, especially of religion and its modern surrogate, Science. If nothing else, these appeals to purported reason show the substantial intellectual investment required to maintain a carnivorous diet in the modern era. I list these claims without refutation or discussion, as space is limited here and the literature on this debate is already vast. (For a recent round: Scully 2002; Marcus 2005; Singer and Mason 2006.)

1. *Divine intent.* God gave us animals to control and dominate (Genesis). Conversely, "I don't believe God or Jesus were vegetarians," a 38-year-old male mechanic says. And, a nursing home worker, aged 24, adds, "I don't believe pigs have souls."
2. *Human intent.* Farm animals are specifically created by modern scientists to be eaten, so we can and *should* eat them.
3. *Natural law, or the biological imperative.* We're all part of the food chain. The "lower" (the pig) gets eaten by the "higher" (that's us). It's the "law of the jungle" – survival of the fittest. "Animals eat each other and it's just as vigorous as when humans eat meat," one 28-year-old trucker argues. "Vegetarians never complain about lions or sharks eating meat. If humans stopped eating meat it would disrupt the food chain."
4. *Tradition.* This is how we have *always* eaten.
5. *Reduction ad absurdum: boundary vagueness.* If you can't kill a cow, why kill a carrot? Where *is* the dividing line between life that deserves protection and life that can be taken? Drawing the line at feelings, an engineer, aged 50, claims, "Animals don't have emotions like humans."
6. *Speciesism: humans come first.* Why worry about animal welfare when there are so many humans who are suffering?
7. *Extremism vs. moderation.* Animal rights people are too extreme, and so is vegetarianism. "Does this guy [Singer] sell flowers at the airport, too?" a 25-year-old male mortician asks. We should eat a "balanced" or "moderate" diet that includes animal products.

While all of these claims can be defended and refuted at length, what's most interesting today is that they do not play a major role in the animal industry's own self-defense. While the animal *rights* lobby may represent minority opinion (at least as seen in the 1000+ Baltimore respondents surveyed by my students), they are an *annoying* minority, and although outnumbered, they have managed to "move the middle" of mainstream thought to the extent that more people *are* concerned about how farm animals are treated. In the more "moderate" animal *welfare* position, animals should be treated better before they are eaten, especially if such humane treatment also results in fewer food-borne illnesses such as *E. coli* and salmonella

(Fox 1997). This generally means less stringent "confinement" before slaughter. That more people are willing to pay a bit more for humanely treated animals is reflected in the growing – but still relatively small – upscale market for "free range" meat, milk, and eggs.[19] Perhaps even more telling is the interest of some fast food giants, including McDonald's, in such products.[20] Of course the motivation is more to curb the use of antibiotics than to improve animals' lives. Like Upton Sinclair, animal rights activists aim for the public's heart but hit its stomach. As the "speciesists" insist, humans do come first – or at least those more affluent humans willing to pay extra for security.

If only the humans who work in the food business had as powerful an advocate as the cows, chickens, and pigs, for surely the impact on food workers is also grave.

In the United States almost 20 percent of the labor force works in the "food and fiber system," which covers every part of the chain from farm to table. While agriculture employs just 2 percent of the US labor force, over 40 percent of the world's workers labor in agriculture – down from over 50 percent in 1980 but still the world's largest employer – and also its poorest. It is no coincidence that the countries with the largest percentage of people devoted to farming are also among the hungriest.[21] Wherever they operate in the food chain, food workers have always paid a huge personal price to feed us. Whether peasants, slaves, meat-packers, fruit-pickers, burger-flippers, or family cooks, their work is physically demanding and often dangerous (think of the heat, dangerous tools, lifting, standing), mind-numbing in its routine, taken for granted, almost always poorly compensated, and yet absolutely indispensable. The inequities in treatment of food workers underlie many systems of exploitation, from slavery and feudalism to patriarchy and imperialism. Thanks to modern packaging, preservatives, transportation, and refrigerated storage, consumers are conveniently distanced from the battered hands that transform the "raw" into the "cooked" (Barndt 2002: 211). The distancing is illusory, however, for as anthropologist Daniel Rothenberg writes in *With These Hands; The Hidden World of Migrant Farmworkers Today*, "Through the simple act of purchasing an orange or a head of lettuce, we are connected with a hidden world of laborers, a web of interconnected lives, with hands on both ends" (Rothenberg 2000: xxii).

Despite our persistent obliviousness to foodwork, some of the most important works of social fiction and muckraking journalism have been devoted to illuminating these producer–consumer connections, including abolitionist Harriet Beecher Stowe's *Uncle Tom's Cabin*, the best-selling novel of the nineteenth century, Upton Sinclair's *The Jungle* (1906), a primary inspiration in the passage of path-breaking food and drug regulations, Pearl Buck's *The Good Earth* (1934) and John Steinbeck's *Grapes of Wrath* (1939) – both Pulitzer- and Nobel Prize-winning portraits of heroic but doomed peasantry, and Edward R. Murrow's CBS News documentary on migrant farmworkers, *Harvest of Shame*, which aired, appropriately enough, the day after Thanksgiving, 1960. While most of these dealt with American-born workers (except Buck, whose Chinese farmers could very well have traveled to the Americas after losing their land), there have also been impressively detailed efforts to document the effects of our globalized supply lines – the "scorching sun" – on distant workers around the globe. As environmental educator Deborah Barndt shows in *Tangled Routes: Women, Work and Globalization on the Tomato Trail* (2002), a seemingly simple ambition to trace the movement of a tomato from Mexican field to Canadian fast food restaurant opens "a Pandora's box. A whole array of other questions comes tumbling out," especially, "Whose hands have planted, cultivated, picked, packed, processed, transported, inspected, sold, and cooked it?" (2). The short answer is: poor people, predominantly female and brown, all invisible and powerless.

A global perspective reveals that entire communities, north and south, rich and poor, overfed and hungry, are entangled in the question of who puts the tomato – and everything else – on our plates. In what might be called a worldwide system of carbohydrate colonialism, vast armies of labor are deployed to supply the extra calories that both nourish and fatten us (Bonanno et al. 1994, McMichael 1994, Lappé et al. 1998, Magdoff et al. 2000).

The system works something like this: governments and banks in the rich North (America, Europe, Japan) lend considerable sums of money to the richest farmers in the South (Latin America, Africa, or South East Asia), who evict small subsistence farmers from their family plots to assemble large, technologically advanced plantations that grow more grain, meat, and luxury crops (whether tomatoes, bananas, coffee, grapes, or pineapples). In the notorious "circle of poison," pesticides manufactured but banned in the North are sent southward to grow these capital-intensive products, poisoning unprotected field workers in the process (Weir and Shapiro 1981; Wright 1990; Murray 1994). (One is tempted to employ the Nazi analogy here, too, as chemicals similar to those used to fumigate crops and farm workers were also applied in the concentration camps.[22])

But while the meat and luxury crops (and their pesticide residues) are eagerly devoured by the affluent North, Southern grain farmers are unable to export their staple crops, as European, American, and Japanese grain farmers are fiercely protected by their own governments; in fact, in North America, "free trade" sends cheap, subsidized American corn south, thereby bankrupting still more peasant farmers in Mexico. The displaced peasants either stay on as exploited farm workers or they may migrate north. (Of Miztecs dispossessed by government-subsidized agricultural modernization, anthropologist Angus Wright asks, "Why is it that people like Ramon" – a farm worker eventually killed by pesticides – "can no longer make a living from their own land and must work instead where they own nothing and control nothing and where their only apparent future is to move on to work in yet some other alien and unfriendly land?" 1990: 9.) Others will stay closer to home, working marginal plots or moving to crowded urban slums where, if they are lucky, they might find work in low-pay factories that export cheap manufactured goods to the North. These goods in turn undersell the aging factories of the North and turn once relatively prosperous blue-collar workers into the "New Poor" who are now reduced to relying on food banks, welfare, and, if lucky, low-paid "service jobs" (Kempf 1997; Poppendieck 1998; Schwartz-Nobel 2002). The job opportunities for Northern-born workers are further diminished by competition from migrants from the South who are willing to work for less in Northern fields, gardens, factories, and construction sites. Meanwhile independent Northern farmers and retailers are undercut by cheaper produce and manufactured goods imported from the South. Main Street loses out to Wal-Mart. Rural children grow up with few opportunities other than to join a military force devoted to protecting the oil supply lines that fuel the whole system.

While hegemonic, this cheap fuel/food system is not entirely rational. Militaries are very expensive to maintain, as is a healthcare system struggling to keep up with the rising costs of those extra calories – and of the extra food-borne microbes that result from unsafe working conditions in remote fields and processing plants. More-over the displaced Southern peasants, however essential as low-paid workers, are increasingly unwelcome in many Northern communities, which are moving to re-strict immigration. Of course, if immigration is restricted, Northern employers will not necessarily raise wages. Rather, pushed by intense global competition to keep costs low, they will probably seek to automate more jobs in the food chain, whether in the fields, meat-packing plants, or at the checkout counter. In the "race to the bottom," workers around the world are sacrificed for cheap food. But the food is not so cheap if it results in downscaled lives, disrupted families, destroyed communities, and dangerous political unrest. If "what goes around comes around," *someone* will eventually pay – but perhaps not on *our* watch. Then again, the "scorching sun" of Arabia (as well as of Mexico, Brazil, the Philippines, Nigeria) is hotter, and closer than we may have thought.

The deferred debt implied here also applies to the environmental damage wrought by the industrial convenience food system. Since this a bill that our children will have to pay, we will examine those environmental costs in the final chapter on the future of food.

Chapter Summary

- "There ain't no such thing as a free lunch."
- In pursuit of cheap food, people have long invaded, colonized or otherwise dominated another. Such "delocalization" has yielded tasty options for Western consumers, who do not have to feel the "scorching sun" under which such foods are produced.
- Personal disgust, not social compassion, drives most campaigns for food industry regulation.
- Threats such as food poisoning are directly linked to the length and complexity of the food chain, so even if we start with our own stomachs, the local quickly becomes global.
- Food safety is a political issue.
- The worst health risks are borne by the poor and disenfranchised.
- Epidemiological statistics indicate that how and what we eat may be threatening our long-term health, and the full costs to us all may be enormous, perhaps even catastrophic.
- For much of history, fatness was identified with prosperity, power, and privilege. Only in the twentieth century did thinness become associated with higher status.
- The diet industry marches in almost perfect sync with some very basic American faiths and notions, yet almost all weight-loss diets fail.
- Some critics argue that the "obesity epidemic" is a "socially constructed," over-hyped "moral panic."
- In addition to affecting our "internal" health, the Nutrition Transition has high "external" costs, especially for animals, workers, and future consumers.
- In what might be called a worldwide system of carbohydrate colonialism, vast armies of labor are deployed to supply the extra calories that both nourish and fatten us.
- What goes around, comes around.

6 THE FUTURE OF FOOD

The debate over the future of modern industrial civilization – and of modern industrial food – is not new to the twenty-first century, when climate change has finally reached the news agenda. For many years, agronomists, politicians, economists, philosophers, and poets have been arguing over whether Progress – defined as more convenience and more meat for more people – is sustainable. Can we keep coming up with new ways to stretch the global food chain, or will the chain ultimately reach its limits and snap? After all, as the ancient proverb goes, "We didn't inherit the land from our fathers; we are borrowing it from our children." If our intensive industrial agriculture depletes the soil, our children will have less natural capital upon which to draw. Continuing the accounting metaphor, ecologist William Vogt warned in 1948 that: "By a lopsided use of applied science, mankind has been living on promissory notes. Now all over the world, the notes are falling due" (Vogt 1948: 248). Must our grandchildren have to pay the bill for our "joyride," as conservationists Guy Irving Burch and Elmer Pendell warned in 1945? (Belasco 2006a: 87). Or worse, are we actually *stealing* from our children, as environmental activist David Brower once suggested: "We're committing grand larceny against our children. Ours is a chain-letter economy in which we pick up early handsome dividends and our children find their mailboxes empty" (McPhee 1971: 82). As we have seen, the "no free lunch" principle was established long before biologist Barry Commoner's 1971 version of the "Four Laws of Ecology":

> Everything is connected to everything else.
> Everything must go somewhere.
> Nature knows best.
> There's no such thing as a free lunch.

The eighteenth-century Iroquois aspired to the same future-minded ethos in their motto, "In our every deliberation we must consider the impact of our decisions on the next seven generations."

But if conservationist thought is deeply rooted, so too is faith that humanity's reach *can* exceed its grasp – that limits exist mainly to be broken. The Bible is famously ambiguous about this debate. On the one hand stands the sobering lesson of Genesis, where divine rage at Adam and Eve's overreaching brings fatal and irretrievable consequences for their children. On the other hand are numerous stories of divine aid that transcends the apparent confines of the moment: the parting of seas, the sweetening of the bitter waters of Marah, the timely delivery of manna from heaven, the blooming of deserts, the miracle of the loaves and fishes, the conversion of water to wine at Cana, the rituals of the Eucharist, and so on. With divine providence, sacred stories suggest, we humans can overcome any obstacles, even mortality. With the Enlightenment, human reason and science took on many of these providential functions. For the late eighteenth-century French mathematician Condorcet, "The perfectibility of man is indefinite ... Nature has set no limits to the realization of our hopes" (Belasco 2006a: 7). In potential, "Man is a godlike being," English radical William Godwin agreed in the early nineteenth century, "Nature never made a dunce" (Belasco 2006a: 22, 81).

Sounding the same humanistic faith 150 years later, journalist Robert Brittain dismissed Vogt's pessimism with a paean to human agricultural ingenuity, *Let There Be Bread* (1952). Note that the Latin translation of his title – *fiat panis* – was also the official slogan of the UN's Food and Agriculture Organization, an institution founded just a few years before with the supremely humanistic faith that hunger could be eliminated once and for all. Revising the Promethean narrative, minus the nasty side effects for that god's own liver, Brittain opened with these selections from Sophocles' *Antigone*:

> He is master of ageless earth, to his own will bending
> The immortal mother of gods by the sweat of his brow ...
> There is nothing beyond his power. His subtlety
> Meeteth all chance, all danger conquereth. (v)

Rejecting the tragic ironies of Sophocles' play, in which just about everyone of consequence winds up dead, Brittain proclaimed, "Man's creative genius is in truth more vigorous than his demon of destructiveness" (9).

Over 200 years before Brittain and the founding of the FAO, Irish satirist Jonathan Swift (1667–1745) had suggested that "Whoever could make two ears of corn, or two blades of grass, to grow upon a spot of ground where only one grew before, would deserve better of mankind, and do more essential service to his country, than the whole race of politicians put together."[1] By Brittain's century, agronomists had accomplished much more than Swift could have imagined. Between 1930 and 1980 alone Iowa corn (maize) yields more than tripled; similar increases worldwide enabled world meat production to more than double per capita just between 1965 and 1985 (Belasco 2006a: 55, 74). Compounding these remarkable gains in productivity, per capita meat consumption *in the developing world* doubled between 1990 and 2005 (Nierenberg 2006; 24). In a famous debate with environmental doomsayer Norman Myers in 1994, boosterish economist Julian Simon observed that in real terms (i.e., adjusted for inflation) American food was much cheaper in 1980 than in 1800, even though the US population had boomed from 5 million to 225 million during that same time. Indeed, population growth actually enabled all that innovation, Simon reasoned, for with more mouths also came more brains and hands. Like Condorcet, Godwin, and Brittain, Simon believed that ingenious humans create more than they consume, and he concluded, "We now have the technology to feed, clothe, and supply energy to an ever-growing population for the next 7 billion years" (Belasco 2006a: 59). Against the pessimists' somber worries about limits, debts, and grand larceny, the giddy optimists see: "The sky's the limit" and "You ain't seen nothin' yet!"

While the debate is ancient, both sides agree that the current challenges are especially daunting. The world's population – the worry of pessimists since Thomas Malthus's famous *Essay on Population* (1798) – is still growing, although the rate of doubling *may* be slowing. In 1800 world population stood at about 1 billion; it took 127 years to double to 2 billion in 1927, about fifty more years to reach 4 billion, but only forty years to double from 3 billion in 1960 to 6 billion in 2000. At current rates, the 2007 population may grow *just* another 50 percent (to 9 billion) in the next forty years.[2] This is relatively good news, considering that some earlier forecasts had envisioned twice that many people by 2050. And birth rates may be slowing even further, for as people become more prosperous, modern, and urban they have fewer children. It is possible that the earth may eventually reach a state of zero population growth – a thought almost inconceivable thirty years ago. According to the "rising tide lifts all boats" aphorism, economic growth will benefit us all.

But is more prosperity necessarily the "cure"? Rich people consume a disproportionate share of the world's resources for food, transportation, leisure, and housing. Regional planners Mathis Wackernagel and William Rees (1996) calculate that the "ecological footprint" of the world's most affluent, best-fed people is at least twenty-five times that of its poorest citizens, and they conclude that it might take three planets for everyone on earth to live at the North American standard. Clearly this is impossible, yet that is the direction the "nutrition transition" seems to be pulling us. While *only* a sixth of the world suffers from food insecurity, the relatively prosperous five-sixths want to consume more meat, dairy foods, beer, and produce. According to the International Food Policy Research Institute (IFPRI), people in developing countries will consume twice as much meat in 2020 as in the 1980s (Nierenberg 2005: 10). Thanks to the worldwide spread of CAFOs (confined animal feeding operations), this meat will be cheap at the checkout counter but loaded with heavy external costs.

Witness the rapid increase of obesity rates in prosperous China. Thanks in part to increased meat and egg consumption, more than 60 million Chinese became obese in the 1990s.[3] But the ecological implications are even more dire. Meat and eggs require a lot of corn and soy. Producing 1 lb of beef requires up to 10 lb of grain (depending on the degree of "marbling"); 1 lb of pork requires 4–6 lb of grain, poultry 2–4 lb, eggs 2–3 lb. While the Chinese have not been eating a great deal of beef, consumption of pork and poultry has soared. China is home to half the world's pigs (Nierenberg 2006: 24). According to IFPRI, by 2020 the Chinese will consume 73 kg of meat a year per capita – up 55 percent from 1993; this compares with an estimate of 90 kg per capita in the West (Nierenberg 2005: 11). Given China's huge population, even small increases have major ecological implications. In *Who Will Feed China?* (1995), economist Lester Brown estimates that if China doubles its egg consumption (to about 200 eggs a year per capita, which is still under the US average of 250), "reaching this goal will take an additional 24 million tons of grain, the amount equal to the total exports of Canada, the world's second-ranking exporter" (48). As the Chinese "move up the food chain" they will also drink more beer, which also requires large quantities of grain (and fresh water – another concern). Between 1981 and 1995 Chinese beer consumption increased from 1 billion liters to 13 billion (11 liters per capita). According to Brown, raising beer consumption just one bottle a year per adult would require 370,000 more tons of grain. Three bottles would take up the entire grain harvest of Norway (51). And doubling the per capita consumption of vegetable oils (mainly corn and soy) to a Japanese standard (which is still half the US level) would require more soybeans than the US exports in a year – and the United States is the world's largest soy exporter (51–52). Of course, with so much extra grain now available in world markets, rising Chinese demand might not have an immediate major impact on food prices (Fuller and Hayes 1998), but Brown raises a legitimate concern about whether we can count on such surpluses in the future. According to the Worldwatch Institute (founded by Brown), per capita grain production has been essentially flat for many years (Halweil 2006: 23). In a globally integrated food system, even a small contraction in grain production could have significant price impacts, especially on the world's poorest people. This can already be seen in the run-up of food prices as grain is converted to ethanol for our cars. Given the relative cheapness of food in affluent countries, the rich can probably afford some inflation – and it might even encourage them to eat less – but the poor have no such margin.[4]

Corn and soy are the basis of the meat-based convenience food diet. Providing all this grain requires large amounts of fuel, water, and soil – and the future of these key "inputs" is in doubt. According to Michael Pollan, growing a bushel of Iowa corn requires somewhere between a quarter and a third of a gallon of oil. This includes the fossil fuels in the fertilizers and pesticides, plus the oil required to fuel the tractor and to dry, store, and transport the corn. This adds up to at least fifty gallons of oil per acre of corn, and that's at the low end of calculations. "Ecologically this is a fabulously expensive way to produce food" (Pollan 2006: 45–46). With prosperity, people also eat more salads and "fresh" produce – much of it trucked across continents, if not also flown across hemispheres. Ecological scientist David Pimentel calculates that it takes 4,600 calories of energy to produce, process, and move a 1lb box of washed *organic* California lettuce to the Eastern United States. That's 57 calories of fossil fuels per calorie of lettuce! (Pollan 2006: 167). In one of those bottom-line estimates that are impossible to verify but that do focus one's mind on the challenges ahead, David and Marcia Pimentel conclude that the American food system requires 10 calories of energy for every calorie of food provided, that it consumes 17 percent of the overall US energy supply, and that if everyone ate the way Americans do, the world would run out of known oil reserves in 13 years (Pimentel and Pimentel 2004). While other estimates are not quite so alarming, few disagree that oil supplies will eventually peak and decline; the quarrel is over which generation will suffer most from spiraling oil prices – more likely the second or third generation than the seventh. And for those of our children who are fighting to protect Middle Eastern oil supply lines, the oil shock is already here. Switching to ethanol *may* reduce oil imports, but it also diverts grain from bellies to gas tanks. In the future will we be competing with our cars for food?

While the oil crisis receives considerable attention – not so much for the long-term impact at the grocery checkout but for the more immediate spike at the gas pump – water shortages may be even more pressing. Agriculture consumes about 80 percent of US fresh water supplies; of this 80 percent goes to animal production – for a multitude of uses, from growing feed grains and watering the animals directly to cleaning the butchered carcasses and flushing away the detritus. Worldwide, agriculture uses 65 percent of the fresh water taken from rivers, aquifers, and lakes; presumably this will increase as the world attempts to grow still more feed grains. If, as the cornucopian optimists claim, we "ain't seen nothin' yet" and the world is going to eat a lot *more* meat, one can hardly begin to imagine the impending draining of water sources. Producing grain is water-intensive: about 1,000 tons of water per ton of harvested grain (Postel 1996: 13). Given the higher feed-to-food conversion ratios of animal products, the nutrition transition costs oceans of water: twenty times more water to supply 500 calories from beef than from rice. Sandra Postel, a water conservationist at the Worldwatch Institute, puts it this way: "The average North American diet takes nearly twice as much water to produce as an equally (or more) nutritious diet low in meat consumption." An American who decided to lower her consumption of animal foods by half would reduce the "water intensity" of her diet by 37 percent (Postel 2005: 45).

These water costs have been well known for a long time. In a clear blow to cornucopian expectations, the 1923 USDA's *Yearbook of Agriculture* suggested that the lack of watered pastures, along with other inputs such as pesticides and fertilizers, would mean that Americans might have to cut back to European levels of meat consumption. Again in 1950 a US presidential commission predicted that scarce water resources might force Americans to reduce livestock consumption by 1975 (Belasco 2006a: 29, 40). Such dire forecasts helped to scare up more government money for massive water projects, which enabled Americans to consume an *additional* 25lb of red meat per capita by 1975 (Brewster and Jacobson 1983: 34). According to one estimate in the mid-1980s, without those dam and irrigation subsidies, Americans would be paying $35 per lb for their burgers (Robbins 1985: 367). In *Diet for a Small Planet*, Frances Moore Lappé quoted two other startling calculations: Counting up all the water used to grow, slaughter, and clean beef cattle, 1lb of hamburger required 2,500 gallons of water to produce. And according to *Newsweek*, "the water that goes into a 1,000 lb steer would float a destroyer" (Lappé 1982: 76). In the three decades since, world meat production has almost doubled, with proportionate increases in water devoted to raising it – 2,400 liters per burger according to a 2006 report.[5] But the world's fresh water supplies have steadily diminished due to climate instability, agricultural reclamation, dams, evaporation, conflict with thirsty cities, the depletion of aquifers, and pollution – some resulting from farm chemicals and animal wastes. About 60 percent of the water used to produce meat goes to cleaning the microbe-rich disassembly line. Following Commoner's principle that "Everything must go somewhere," much of that water is released into waterways; a single slaughterhouse in Hong Kong produces 5 million liters of wastewater every day (Nierenberg 2005: 27).

Adding up all these water costs in 1996, Postel estimated that meeting the grain requirements of the world's likely population in 2025 would require finding twelve more Nile Rivers' worth of fresh water, or fifty-six times the annual flow of the Colorado River – the primary and endangered supplier of water to southwestern US cities and farms (15). In 2005 she upped the estimated needs for 2030 to twenty-four more Niles. A 50 percent reduction in American livestock consumption would save the equivalent of fourteen Colorado Rivers (Postel 2005: 13, 46). At present, saving just one Colorado River would be miraculous.[6] Clearly, such calculations do not allow for a worldwide nutrition transition to the current North American standard. Even if we had endless petroleum supplies, water scarcity alone would seem to set a rather severe limit on the global growth potential of McDonald's.

And then there is the primary agricultural input, soil, the indispensable medium through which plants convert solar energy to human food. As any gardener or farmer will attest, soil is not simply "dirt." In addition to water, soil contains absolutely essential rocks and volcanic minerals, live and decaying organic matter, microbes, gases, as well as numerous components yet to be evaluated. We understand amazingly little about the topsoil that roots and nourishes our plants, but this we do know: it takes hundreds of years to build and deposit an inch of it, but only a single storm to blow or wash it away. And thanks to overgrazing and monoculture – the technologically intense, repetitive growing system of industrial agriculture – it has been disappearing at alarming rates. In the 1970s Frances Moore Lappé reported that Iowa was losing two bushels of topsoil for every bushel of corn harvested; the USDA attributed a quarter of all US soil erosion to corn production alone – almost all of it used for livestock (Lappé 1982: 80). Thirty years later, nature writer Peter Warshall claimed that US farmland was losing topsoil "an average of seventeen times faster than it is formed" – and this was after expensive soil conservation policies that had cut soil erosion rates significantly since Lappé's book had appeared (Warshall 2002: 172). In 1993, the World Resources Institute estimated that since 1945 the world had lost over 10 percent of its vegetated land to soil degradation – the equivalent of China and India combined (Tribe 1994: 63). In the long run the picture is worse: Over 60 percent of the world's land brought under irrigation during the past 300 years suffers from the effects of salinization (the build-up of toxic salts in the soil); 20 percent of this irrigated land has been abandoned altogether (Rozanov, Targulian, Orlov 1990: 210).

Modern concern about the soil crisis dates back at least to the mid-nineteenth century, when the loss of Western soil fertility preoccupied a wide range of reformers, from chemist Justus von Liebig to socialist Karl Marx (Foster and Magdoff 2000). In the 1920s, over-plowing of wheat and feed grains eventually produced the American Dust Bowl, which geographer Georg Borgstrom termed one of the three greatest ecological blunders in human history, along with the deforestation of upland China around 3000 BCE and the overgrazing of the Mediterranean region in the classical era (Worster 1979: 4). Famous photographs of Great Plains farmhouses buried in blowing sand inspired ecological jeremiads warning that agricultural overproduction was dooming modern civilization to the same tragic fate as other once mighty societies that had over-plowed, over-irrigated, or overgrazed their soil – for example, the Sumer of the Near East, the Maya and Anasazi of America (Sears 1959, Goudie 1990). For geographer Carl Sauer, the destruction of soil seemed a classic case of stealing from one's children. "A considerable part of the growth of the nineteenth century and of our own time has been by a process of skimming the cream from the land" (Sauer 1937: 16). Conservationists also invoked the now familiar metaphors of accounting with which this chapter opened. According to Sauer, "The agricultural surpluses of the US have been produced, it would seem, by the dissipation of land capital" (18). "The only way to treat the soil is like a bank account," plant geneticist

Edward East pronounced, "husband it carefully by proper farming and make a deposit once in awhile" (1924: 186). Although the Dust Bowl was a wake-up call for soil conservation, the great plow-up continued unabated worldwide, with even grimmer consequences for Africa, Asia, and Latin America. So along with memorable black-and-white photos of the Dirty Thirties, we are now confronted by full-color images of the Sahel, Aral Sea, and northeast Brazil.

Illustrating Commoner's first law – "Everything's connected" – the soil problem shows how agriculture is an integrated feedback loop of actions and unintended consequences. As humans do more to improve fertility and productivity, the worse some other problem becomes. Dryland farming – the source of about 60 percent of the world's food crops – is cheap but has low yields, is easily over-plowed, and is very vulnerable to wind erosion. Irrigation raises productivity (20 percent of the world's farmland produces 40 percent of its crops) and reduces wind damage but increases both local and international conflicts over water rights. Irrigation requires costly dams, pipes, sprinklers, valves, pumps, and energy (to run the pumps). It may also deplete nutrients, drain aquifers, foster salinization, waste water through evaporation and leakage, cause desertification of neighboring land and further run-off. Eroded sediments and nutrients clog waterways and kill wildlife down-stream, at tremendous economic and biological cost. To make up for lost nutrients, farmers can apply either animal or chemical fertilizers. Thanks to industrial animal production, animal manures abound but are tricky to use correctly on a large scale. Manures are not evenly available and may be full of toxic heavy metals if the animals were fed pesticide-sprayed grain. Chemical fertilizers are more convenient but are expensive, require fossil fuels to manufacture and apply, and degrade soil structure, thereby furthering erosion. Both forms pollute water resources, underground and downstream. And in the classic colonial model, farmers who abandon degraded soils to seek out new land may destroy forests, kill wildlife, and fight with herdsmen. Or, to connect with the labor issue discussed in the previous chapter, they may become "environmental refugees" ripe for exploitation in large industrial plantations and sweatshops – e.g., the Okies of John Steinbeck's *Grapes of Wrath* (1939). If anything, these problems are worse in developing nations, where tropical ecosystems are more fragile and government oversight is weak. Thus of the 900 million hectares[7] of drylands degraded by water and wind in the 1990s, over two-thirds were in Africa, Asia, and South America.[8]

But what happens when there is no more "virgin land" to conquer? The era of "colonize–destroy–move on" is over (Hardin 1993: 95). While some surveys estimate that the world has twice as much potential farmland as it currently uses, most of it is in wetlands and forests that, for ecological reasons, should not be converted. And even this would be inadequate to provide for a global nutrition transition.

Geographer Vaclav Smil estimates that to feed everyone an animal-intensive Western diet it would take 67 percent more agricultural land than the world has (Smil 2000: 37, Singer and Mason 2006: 233). Yet we cannot even count on retaining *current* farmlands. In many areas it is more profitable to convert farmland to roads, cities, malls, and suburban subdivisions. Even the most dedicated farmers in North America, Europe, and Japan are tempted to "grow houses" rather than cheap feed grains. Developing countries are also converting existing grain lands to other uses – e.g., factories, housing, and transportation, as well as the more ecologically sound orchards, forests, and ponds. In the 1990s, the Chinese population grew by over 10 percent but its farmland decreased by 3 percent (Smil 2000: 34). "After thousands of years of expansion," Worldwatch researcher Gary Gardner notes, "the amount of grain land under cultivation worldwide peaked [in 1981], topping 732 million hectares. Between 1981 and 1995, in roughly a mirror image of its steady climb, harvested grain area fell by 7.6 percent," before rebounding to 695 million hectares in 1996 (Gardner 1996: 8). By 2002, according to Lester Brown, there were 670 million hectares of grain land.[9] Less grain land means more expensive meat. Here again is a major obstacle to the nutrition transition and to conventional notions of Progress.

SCENARIOS

So where does all this lead us? Given these constraints, how will the world feed itself in the future, especially if it wants Progress? Is it hopeless, or are there things we can do? Stiff challenges are by no means a reason to despair. In fact, conjuring up one's worst nightmare can be the first step toward avoiding it. This may be one of the primary reasons why we relish scary stories: to keep them from happening (Belasco 2006a: 119–146). Even the gloomiest pessimist of them all, Thomas Malthus, ended his otherwise depressing 1798 forecast of perennial overpopulation, famine, and food wars with this bracing call for action: "Evil exists in the world not to create despair but activity. We are not patiently to submit to it, but to exert ourselves to avoid it" (Malthus 1985 [1798]: 217).

To avoid disaster, we need to predict it. Science fiction aside, how do we go about making predictions? In speculating about the future, professional futurists are wary of declarations such as, "In 2020 the world will ..." Such single-track forecasts tend to ignore too many of the unknowns, dependent variables, human foibles, and surprises that determine how things actually turn out. Furthermore, they may underestimate the choices that we can make to determine the future. The future is invented in the present; it is the outgrowth of current decisions.

To allow for options, futurists often develop alternate "scenarios" that suggest what *might* happen *if* we choose (or not) to devote resources to pursuing a particular path. Given the absolute necessity of food and the immensity of the food industry, there are dozens, perhaps hundreds of scenarios out there, for the future of food is the concern of countless businesses, government agencies, universities, think tanks, and non-governmental organizations. At the risk of oversimplifying, I will suggest two different scenarios for how we might feed ourselves. Each is optimistic in its own way, but each depends on very different assumptions about human interests, values, and will.

Box 6.1. Two Scenarios for the Future

The food supply of the future will be determined by the way that humanity addresses several mounting environmental crises, especially climate change, soil erosion, rising petroleum prices, and water shortages. In this exercise, please imagine two alternate diets for your grandchildren, fifty years from now, one for a future based on "technological fixes" to these resource challenges, the other based on "anthropological fixes." For each scenario, describe three full meals (breakfast, lunch, dinner). Using the components of "cuisine" discussed in Chapter 2, page 15ff., include details such as:

- Basic foods.
- Preparation techniques.
- Predominant flavor principles.
- Manners.
- Infrastructure: Where do these foods come from and how do they get from farm to table?

THE TECHNOLOGICAL FIX: BUSINESS AS USUAL

According to this scenario, by harnessing technological invention to profit-seeking free enterprise, humanity has already beaten the odds and proved Thomas Malthus wrong. Viewing population growth and environmental constraints in 1798, Malthus predicted that food supplies would soon run short of demand, leading to famine and misery for the mass of humanity, and to a rather skimpy "Asiatic" (low-meat) diet for the fortunate few. The Malthusian warning has been recycled numerous times in the past 200 years – most recently by earnest environmentalists Paul Ehrlich, Lester

Brown, and David Pimentel (Belasco 2006a). But so far at least human ingenuity has produced more grain, and thus more meat, milk, and eggs, than we can consume, even as the world's population has increased six-fold since Malthus's day. For this the Malthusians might actually be thanked, for their scary scenarios inspired the agricultural research that has held off the widespread shortages that Malthus feared.

The technological fix[10] has several key assumptions: First, human wants are limitless and should not be curtailed – nor should social structures be reformed to encourage personal restraint or to redistribute resources. In food terms, this means that if everyone wants to move up the food chain to a convenience-based diet rich in animal protein, "fresh" produce, prepared meals (whether restaurant or carryout), and other luxuries such as beer, soft drinks, and chocolate, then so be it. The more the merrier. We do not need government ("the national nanny"), nutritionists ("the food police"), or environmentalists ("tree huggers") to tell us to lighten up. Instead we should be free to pursue our individual tastes and cravings, wherever they lead. Infinite needs can be met by humanity's infinite creativity, especially if we let markets work. Given the right economic incentives, there will always be someone who will figure out a way to produce more food. Just before Malthus expressed his worries about overpopulation, the philosopher Condorcet predicted that the demand for more food would encourage scientists to investigate "the feasibility of manufacturing animal and vegetable substances artificially, [and] the utilization of substances which were wasted" (Manuel 1965: 93). And a hundred years later, in 1894, French chemist Marcelin Berthelot suggested that "the long evolution" of human innovation would by the year 2000 lead to a "tablet of factory-made beefsteak" synthesized from coal (Dam 1894).

According to this technological paradigm, anything man-made, including food, is "artificial" by definition. Just as the dictionary offers "art" as the antonym of "nature," food technologists have long insisted that "nature" is not our ally in this fight to produce more, so it must be fought and dominated at every turn. In fact, natural foods can be deadly – e.g., aflatoxin in peanuts, tuberculosis in raw milk, nitrates in celery – and "natural" methods of farming are insufficient to fight off the weeds, bugs, and other pests that want a hefty bite of our crops. Nor is the past much of a guide, for in this modernist worldview, human "tradition" means plagues, pestilence, and pellagra.

Over the course of agricultural evolution there have been numerous technological fixes for our demographic and ecological dilemmas: for example, better seeds, plows, barns, harvesters, pumps, fertilizers, pesticides, refrigerators, bigger and faster tractors, trucks, trains and planes, and so on. While some of these inventions were developed by small-scale farmers, the new technologies required to feed the future are not cheap or simple. Paying for their research, development, and maintenance requires large investments at every stage of the food chain. Despite agrarian sentiments, bigger has been better for almost a century. For example, in an influential 1929 book, *Too Many Farmers*, farm journalist Wheeler McMillen proclaimed, "Enormous possibilities for improving the economic and social status of people engaged in agriculture lie in the application of the corporation to farming … Corporations, by supplying capital and all the tools of production, and requiring of each employee only that he use the gifts nature has bestowed upon him, bring out the best of man's competence" (McMillen 1929: 303, 318). If food production is dominated by giant corporations such as Archer Daniels Midland, Monsanto, and Cargill, that's inevitable. Or as US Secretary of Agriculture Ezra Taft Benson told farmers in the 1950s, the decade of agriculture's greatest technological leaps, "Get big or get out" (Fite 1981: 102–117). To this, Nixon-era agriculture secretary Earl Butz added, "Adapt or die." This applied to the Third World as well. Even though the famous "Green Revolution" of the 1960s and 1970s was designed to help poor countries feed themselves, these high-yield seeds worked best when cultivated with the costly chemicals and tractors that only the richest farmers could afford.

And now perhaps our most ambitious – and most expensive – technological hopes focus on breakthroughs in genetic engineering, microtechnology, and nanotechnology. Through what historian Joseph Amato calls "the control of miniature things" – genes, microbes, molecules, and other forms of "dust" – humans can direct evolution (Amato 2000: 108). And they can do so more efficiently, for the new biotechnologies are quicker and more precise than older forms of genetic selection, which required a laborious, multi-generational process of cross-breeding and growing-out.

Armed with their new "smart" tools, scientists will overcome, and perhaps undo the environmental damage wrought by earlier generations. For example, plants can be redesigned to resist the new diseases fostered by industrial monoculture and even to flourish in salinized soils, overgrazed deserts, deforested jungles, polluted air, or eroded plains. If Global Warming proceeds as anticipated, vast new frontiers of Arctic grain land will be opened up for exploitation, while low-lying areas may be flooded. In response, biotechnology may create plants best suited for the special growing conditions of northern tundra and southern wetlands. Corn, wheat, rice, and soy can also be engineered to grow faster with fewer dangerous pesticides, or in Monsanto's Roundup-Ready version, to grow well only when doused in particular pesticides sold by the same company that makes the seed. Such advances will, of course, cost farmers a substantial premium. Animals, too, can be reprogrammed to withstand the toxic bacteria of factory farms and to require less corn and soy per pound of usable protein. Faced with the near-collapse of world fisheries, scientists can develop new varieties of salmon, shrimp, and tilapia that grow 50 percent faster and bigger in highly capitalized fish farms. And, jumping ahead a bit, through nanotechnology proteins can be synthesized from the molecular level up, using whatever organic source is cheapest and most available – corn, rice, brewery yeast, even sawdust – producing tasty, healthy, meat-like foods far more efficiently than even the most up-to-date CAFO, which must still depend on live animals for meat.

As an added side benefit for conservationists, the "bio-refineries" of the future will require less space than conventional dirt farming, thus releasing land back to wilderness. For example, the title of a 1994 report financed by pro-agribusiness interests asked, *How Much Land Can Ten Billion People Spare for Nature?* The answer was quite a lot, with high-tech "smart farming" (Waggoner 1994). That same year, a similar link was suggested in the title of agricultural scientist Derek Tribe's brief for biotechnology, *Feeding and Greening the World* (Tribe 1994).[11] This "back to nature" benefit of chemistry was also voiced exactly a hundred years earlier by Marcelin Berthelot, who predicted that synthetic chemistry – which he termed "spiritual chemistry"—would return humanity to pre-Fall Eden, where still-innocent Adam and Eve did not have to scratch the earth for a meager living. "If the surface of the earth ceases to be divided and I must say disfigured by the geometrical devices of agriculture, it will regain its natural verdure of woods and flowers" (Dam 1894: 312). And halfway between Berthelot and Tribe, chemist Jacob Rosin argued that industrial synthesis of food would free the landscape "from its dedication to food production. A new way of life will emerge. Crowded cities will disappear, and the earth will be transformed into a Garden of Eden" (Rosin and Eastman 1953: 57).

Technological ingenuity may also transform the rest of the food chain. Auto-mated factories and "just-in-time" supply chains will be both more productive and also more "responsive" to shifting consumer demands. In the global supermarket "fresh," tasty, and interesting foods will speed almost anywhere in the world thanks to "green" ships, planes, and trucks that will use less energy and produce less pollution. New types of packaging will require much less paper or plastic, will automatically monitor freshness, and will biodegrade completely when empty. Supermarkets will be redesigned around themes that will enable shoppers to build complete meals effortlessly; thus an "Italian" section might link pastas with appropriate sauce, cheese, sausage, bread, salad, and gelato. Computerized terminals will offer shoppers information on nutrition, recipes, and perhaps even the geographic sources of products. Shoppers with "smart cards" will not have to find a terminal, as their encoded cards will automatically match past purchases, medical history, and personal needs with particular goods that will be loaded into "smart carts" designed to monitor sales and make "helpful" suggestions along the way. Needless to say, since lower labor costs translate into lower food prices and higher profits, grocers will also "robotize" warehouses, service kiosks, shelf restocking, and checkout, thereby furthering the deskilling and de-unionization of blue-collar work – and providing more low-waged jobs for displaced peasants. Consumers may not even have to leave their homes to shop or to take out the garbage, as other "smart kitchen" technologies will link supermarket delivery services directly to fridge, package, microwave, waste disposal, and sewer.

Through the precise engineering of "functional" foods, the bodies of consumers can be manipulated to absorb needed medicines and nutrients without affecting basic tastes, habits, and needs. Snack foods will *finally* "taste good" *and* be "good for you," as a host of new sweeteners, fats, and spices will allow us to indulge ourselves without guilt. No pain, and no weight gain either. Some foods will be designed to control metabolism so that consumers will actually lose pounds by downing them. For the ultimate in no-sweat convenience, we will down our scientifically fortified "smart drinks" designed to improve memory, alertness, and analytical sharpness, all without any effort or thought (Belasco 2006a).

In this pure, engineer's fantasy of the Gee Whiz, there is no real conflict within the identity–convenience–responsibility triangle (see page 7), for the demand for convenience *is* the essence of human identity, and it is through corporate research and development that this need is met most responsibly. But, as we have seen in earlier chapters, engineers do not run food companies. Rather, marketers have long known that technological fixes alone are not accepted unless they are guised in *fantasies* that are less high-tech than historic – the sixth of the Eight Fs of Fast Food Marketing (see page 69). The wholly artificial meal pills, ethers, and tubed food of earlier science fiction will not appeal, however efficient, for modern consumers are nostalgic for the premodern. Therefore, all of these new engineered foods will have to look and taste like the foods that *someone's* grandma made, if not in reality then at least in Golden Age sitcoms, the glossy pages of *Saveur*, or on the Food Channel. This longing for "authentic tradition" also forms the core of a very different scenario for the future of food, the anthropological fix.

THE ANTHROPOLOGICAL FIX: BACK TO THE FUTURE

In the anthropological fix[12] we redesign people's values, not their gizmos, to meet the challenges of feeding the future. Like the technological fix, this scenario has faith in "smartness" – but not of the brisk and snappy Gee Whiz variety. For guidance and inspiration it looks to traditional wisdom, not modernist bravura. Even its critique of the technological fix is phrased in somewhat antiquarian terms. Biotechnology is framed as *hubris* – a Promethean defiance of limits and laws that will lead to the dystopian scenarios of science fiction classics such as *Frankenstein* (Mary Shelley), *Brave New World* (Aldous Huxley), and *The Island of Dr. Moreau* (H. G. Wells). Titles like *A Garden of Unearthly Delights* (Mather 1996), *Farmageddon* (Kneen 1999), *Lords of the Harvest* (Charles 2001), *Against the Grain* (Lappé and Bailey 1998), *Shattering* (Fowler and Mooney 1990), and *The Last Harvest* (Raeburn 1995) suggest that modernist tinkering may bring divine retribution. On the other hand, the covers of books advocating more old-fashioned food production and distribution soothe us with time-tested pastoral images: *Enduring Seeds* (Nabhan 1989), *Simple in Means, Rich in Ends* (Devall 1988), *A Continuous Harmony* (Berry 1970), *At Nature's Pace* (Logsdon 1994), and *Meeting the Expectations of the Land* (Jackson et al. 1984).

The anthropological fix follows the romantic resistance to the Industrial Revolution. At about the same time as Mary Shelley was speculating about the dangers of scientific manipulation (in *Frankenstein*, 1818) her fellow romantics were advocating, and sometimes even practicing, a simpler life rich in natural foods, and light in the animal foods, caffeinated stimulants, foreign ("Arabian") spices, and "adulterated" commercial products that were already being welcomed, in an early version of the nutrition transition, by contemporary urban consumers. Soon after Mary and her husband Percy declared their vegetarian rebellion, American food reformer Sylvester Graham put home-baked whole wheat bread, raw vegetables, and vigorous temperance at the center of full-scale rejection of modernist science and consumer culture. For Graham, "The simpler, plainer, and more natural the food ... the more healthy, vigorous, and long lived the body" (Slotnick 2004: 574). Biographer Stephen Nissenbaum notes that Graham was particularly enamored of the image of the bread-baking agrarian mother, whom he idealized as the essence of restraint, care, and discipline – the very opposite of contemporary city life, which he saw as hedonistic, materialistic, and debilitating. The contrast was embodied in his rejection of commercially baked bread, which according to Nissenbaum "was only a metaphor of the Jacksonian marketplace – a place of fevered chaos, laden with products manufactured by invisible men and corrupted with invisible poisons." To be sure, Graham's agrarian/matriarchal nostalgia was not based on his family background, which was quite dysfunctional and unloving. "It is, therefore, a revealing irony that Sylvester Graham tried to romanticize the secure family life he had never known" (Nissenbaum 1988: 17–19). In this, Graham anticipated our sentimentality about "old-fashioned" home cooking and the purported decline of family meals.

And Graham himself was part of a much larger nineteenth-century back-to-nature movement that produced hundreds of utopian experiments in rural communal living. Like so many visionaries, including Marcelin Berthelot, these dreamers sought a new Eden, but through a scaling back of human ambitions, consumption, and impact, rather than through Berthelot's "spiritual chemistry" of synthesis and mechanization. From the agrarian utopias of William Morris in England and Bronson Alcott in Fruitlands, Massachusetts, it was a pretty straight leap, a hundred years later, to the hippy country communes of Findhorn, Scotland, and Morningstar Ranch, California. And these communities in turn nurtured the ideas and activists of the sustainable food movement, the leading edge of the anthropological fix (Belasco 2006b).

The primary components of this fix are ideological, as they require a considerable downscaling of futuristic anticipation. Instead of the bright and shiny technological utopia of much science fiction, the sustainable vision is more modest, even disappointing. In *Woman on the Edge of Time* (1976) Marge Piercy's heroine Connie Ramos expresses this sense of letdown when she is transported to the countercultural hamlet of Mattapoisett, Massachusetts, in the year 2137. Instead of the "rocket ships, skyscrapers ... glass domes over everything" and "robots on the march" of pulp sci fi, she glimpses a "Podunk future" of "little no account buildings" made of "scavenged old wood, old bricks and stones ... wildly decorated and overgrown with vines." A tough New Yorker with distant Mexican roots, Connie feels like she is "stuck back home on the farm. Peons again! Back on the same old dung-heap with ten chickens and a goat" (68–70). But like other visitors to such Ecotopian futures (Callenbach 1975; Starhawk 1993), Connie soon discovers that this is no "wetback" slum but rather a deliberate outcome of the cost-accounting, multi-generational conscientious consumption expressed earlier in this chapter. Here the goal of "living lightly on the earth" guides every decision.

Thinking deliberately, carefully, *responsibly* about the consequences of current actions, the conscientious consumer will want to select products that are green for the environment, fair for workers and producers, and humane for animals. Production of such foods will likely entail fewer inputs of petrochemical energy, but considerably more of the human variety – attention, sweat, care. Mindful of the ecological costs of animal food production, this consumer will want to eat "lower down the food chain," that is closer to the vegetable sources of calories and protein. This conscious rejection of the perquisites of progress, i.e., the nutrition transition, does not necessarily entail a completely vegetarian diet, however. Rejecting just the grain-fed products of CAFOs, and seeking out range-fed animals will save considerable amounts of fuel, water, and soil. But here, too, consumers will need to redesign their expectations, for such products may take longer to cook, be tougher to chew, and will certainly be pricier. They may also be less convenient, for consumers will be more aware of the high external costs of well-packaged prepared foods. Eating "lower down the food chain" entails more cooking "from scratch," along with more scratch farming (Halweil 2004; Gussow 2001; Petrini 2001; Pollan 2006; Singer and Mason 2006).

Box 6.2. Develop a New Sustainable Product

Background: You are part of an insurgent group of food marketers who are breaking away from the Gigantic Food Corporation (a division of Carcinogenic Tobacco — see Box 4.2), because you are fed up with the practices of the conventional food industry. Instead, you'd like to develop a company that practices *sustainable* food production and distribution but also succeeds in a mass market. While you hope eventually to have a full product line, you're going to start with just one product that will compete directly with the tasty morsels proposed in the earlier simulation. Your challenge is to concoct and name a new convenience food product using sustainably produced ingredients, which you must locate, and to sketch out a marketing campaign announcing the new product.

Guidelines

Ingredients: Since you're confronting Gigantic's new product head-on, you want to invent a product that uses similar materials — but these need to be *sustainably produced*:

■ Tomatoes, green peppers, string beans; ground meat (beef or poultry).
■ Wheat flour, vegetable oil.
■ Appropriate seasonings, cheese.
■ Environmentally friendly packaging.

Sources: To be sustainable, these ingredients must meet several criteria:

■ Relocalized: seasonal and regional.
■ Lower "down the food chain" than most products.
■ Humane to animals and food workers.
■ Healthy for consumers.
■ Production does not waste resources or harm the environment.
■ Affordable for low-income families.

Following the same directions as given in Box 4.2, discuss the engineering, marketing, and ethical challenges of designing such a product. Is it possible? Are there any comparable products currently on the market?

Central to the sustainable future is a rejection of the 24/7 expectations of the global supermarket — the celebration of "choice." Instead of demanding any food from anywhere at any time, responsible consumers will want to eat locally and seasonally. In the temperate zones this means no strawberries or tomatoes in winter, no oranges in summer, and perhaps no pineapples *ever*. In return for giving up the unlimited options of the modern market, we will get food that may be fresher, healthier, and safer. Since food will not have to travel thousands of miles from farm to fork, it will retain more of its original taste, appearance, and nutrients. Energy costs will be reduced, and regional farm communities will be revived, with a resultant rebirth of the agrarian values thought to be lost in the urban-industrial age. Farmers' markets, cooperatives, and local shops will be particularly important in this future, for food producers and consumers will once again know each other. As Sylvester Graham suggested long ago, if your farmer, baker, or butcher knows you, she is less likely to poison or cheat you. And if you know your farmer you are more likely to be sympathetic to the environmental, labor, and economic challenges of food production. This reduction in "distancing" will thus reduce the alienation, ignorance, and blame shifting fostered by the global food chain.

While such "relocalization" will reshape the food system and landscape in very material ways, it depends, again, on a fundamental redesign of values and hopes. Consumers will need to accept produce that looks less "perfect," tougher meat, fewer options overall in the supermarket. Without the economies of scale achieved by Fordist mass production, prices will be higher, although enlightened consumers will take satisfaction in paying more of the "true costs" of their food. Of course, being conscientious will require the energy, literacy, will, and *time* to research these costs and to learn lost skills such as growing your own and cooking from scratch. Finding that extra time will be a major challenge in an attention-deficit culture that sees itself as perennially rushed and exhausted. Positing a radical reworking of personal routines, social structures, and economic calculations, the anthropological fix is considerably more utopian than the technological variety, which "fixes" our tools, not our ambitions.

These are extreme scenarios, of course, neither of which will "win" in its entirety. Nor will we likely experience the neo-Malthusian alternative of complete "overshoot and collapse" (Meadows et al. 1992), at least not in the richest countries. Rather the real future will be more complex and mixed, as it always is. We can already see many attempts to splice technological and anthropological fixes. For example, the European Union angles to standardize food quality across the continent and to promote microtechnological research while also accommodating its citizens' interest in *terroir*, artisanal cheeses, and Slow Food. China embraces McDonald's, biotechnology, and globalization while also preserving a food production system based on decentralized, small-scale, family-run businesses. In the United States we see the paradox of mega-retailers like Wal-Mart selling organic foods, while organic food retailer Whole Foods adapts the "smart" corporate expansion strategies of Wal-Mart. And consumers struggle to find foods that are *both* convenient *and* "authentic," quick *and* virtuous. Fast food chains continue to grow, but so do tiny restaurants, many of them operated by chefs committed to finding sustainably produced local foods.

There is no doubt that the food industry, which incorporates an enormous variety of enterprises, from multinational grain merchants and processors to microbreweries and bread "boutiques," can provide options that straddle these conflicting drives. But perhaps the best place for the individual consumer to begin to reconcile the contradictory tugs of identity, convenience, and responsibility is in the kitchen. As I tell my students at the end of my food course, if you want to create a better future, start by learning to cook. In our quick-and-easy age, it's one of the more subversive things you can do, for when you cook you take control of a piece of the food chain. Moreover, you may start to wonder how the food got to your kitchen – and that's a really good question.

Chapter Summary

- The debate over the future of modern industrial civilization — and of modern industrial food — is not new to the twenty-first century.
- Conservationists have long worried about the limits of technology and the earth's carrying capacity, while cornucopians have had much greater faith in the ability of human ingenuity to overcome all obstacles.
- There is little doubt that, over the past two centuries, world agricultural productivity has increased much more rapidly than almost anyone anticipated. The Malthusian nightmare that population will outgrow the food supply has not happened — yet.
- Even if population growth levels off, economic growth may endanger the world's resources, for rich people consume a disproportionate share of the world's resources for food, transportation, leisure, and housing.
- The external costs of the Nutrition Transition (more meat, alcohol, and luxury foods) are very high.
- Corn and soy are the basis of the meat-based convenience food diet. Providing all this grain requires large amounts of fuel, water, and soil.
- Illustrating Barry Commoner's first law — "Everything's connected" — food production is an integrated feedback loop of actions and unintended consequences.
- The future is invented in the present; it is the outgrowth of current decisions.
- To avoid disaster we need to predict it.
- The technological fix scenario assumes that by harnessing human inventiveness to profit-seeking free enterprise, we can beat the odds and continue to spread the Nutrition Transition across the globe.
- In the pure, engineer's fantasy of the technological fix there is no real conflict within the identity–convenience–responsibility triangle, for the demand for convenience *is* the essence of human identity, and it is through corporate research and development that this need is met most responsibly.
- In the anthropological fix we redesign people's values, not their gizmos, to meet the challenges of feeding the future.
- The real future may entail a splicing of both technological and anthropological fixes.

QUESTIONS FOR ESSAYS AND CLASS DISCUSSION

CHAPTER I   WHY STUDY FOOD?

- How did agriculture remake the world?
- How is food "fundamental, fun, frightening, and far-reaching?" (Rozin 1999).
- How do your colleagues react when you tell them you are studying food?
- Why the more recent interest in food studies? How is studying food both "respectable" and "subversive"?
- Do modern food consumers tend to take food for granted? If so, why?
- How is food "gross"?
- Is food still considered more a concern for women than men?
- In determining consumer decisions, why do considerations of convenience tend to outweigh those of responsibility?
- Why is meat so highly prized in so much of the world?

CHAPTER 2   IDENTITY: ARE WE WHAT WE EAT?

- Think of your own family as a mini-society, with its own distinctive "cuisine." What are your family's basic foods, flavor principles, preparation techniques, manners, and supply system?
- Conventional wisdom holds that the family dinner is in "decline." Is this true in your case? In what new ways do modern families find time to eat together?
- Given the size and diversity of the United States, is it meaningful to talk of an "American cuisine"? Indeed, is it meaningful to talk of *any* national cuisine?
- How do *you* eat an Oreo?

- Assess the strengths and weaknesses of using food memoirs (*madeleines*) as social or historical data. Is there a disparity between what people *say* (representation) and what they actually *do* (behavior)? And how accurate are our memories anyway?
- How are food memories exploited for profit and power?
- What are the limits of the "You are what you eat" axiom? In what ways might your food choices *not* reveal who you are?

CHAPTER 3   THE DRAMA OF FOOD: DIVIDED IDENTITIES

- Thinking about love songs today, is food as eroticized now as it was back in the 1920s and 1930s? Have food and sex become disconnected? If so, why?
- To what extent do women control food and to what extent does food control women?
- Is "home cooking" overrated? Conversely, might fast food be underappreciated?
- How have convenience foods "liberated" women?
- If women stopped cooking, what would be lost? Gained?
- What would it take to get men to do more family "foodwork"?
- Should a true feminist be a vegetarian?
- At one time, women on a first date were advised not to eat too much in front of men. Why? Is this still true?

CHAPTER 4   CONVENIENCE: THE GLOBAL FOOD CHAIN

- Do consumers want convenience because they are too "lazy"?
- Many people claim they lack time to cook, but isn't this a poor excuse? Is it *that* hard to cook?
- Should convenience foods be celebrated or deplored?
- Why is the food industry often less than forthcoming in revealing its processes and practices?
- Could you sleep at night working for a major food corporation? Defend yourself using both "inside" and "outside" perspectives.
- To what extent do the "Eight Fs" still guide convenience food marketing today?
- Why do most new products fail?
- How do consumers "glocalize" imported foods? Is this good or bad?

CHAPTER 5   RESPONSIBILITY: WHO PAYS FOR DINNER?

- *How* much depends on dinner?
- Which myth is more compelling, Prometheus or Cockaigne?
- Noting the wide outrage after the 1906 publication of *The Jungle*, Upton Sinclair complained, "I aimed for their hearts, but hit their stomachs." Was this a bad thing?
- Why is it difficult to get an accurate accounting of the extent and costs of food-borne illness?
- How is food safety largely a "political" issue?
- How much are people willing to pay for safer, healthier, more responsibly produced food?
- To what extent is fatness the fault and responsibility of individual eaters? To what extent is it a larger social, economic, and political problem? Who *should* pay the medical costs of obesity?
- To what extent is fatness a particularly "American" problem?
- Is it true that anyone can lose weight if s/he wants to? Why is "dieting" generally futile?
- Might the "obesity epidemic" be overstated?
- What do we owe the billions of animals who provide our milk and cheese, eggs, meat, feathers, hides, and wool? What do we owe the human workers who feed us? And how much more are we willing to pay to minimize their suffering and sacrifice?
- Why does the quote from Isaac Bashevis Singer's *The Penitent* (Box 5.2) elicit such strong reactions?
- How do you react to the seven defenses of meat eating listed on page 99?

CHAPTER 6   THE FUTURE OF FOOD

- Pondering the debate over the future of the food supply, which position is more persuasive: optimism or pessimism?
- Which trend is more worrisome: population growth or economic growth?
- If natural resources are limited, which is the more realistic scenario the future: the technological fix or the anthropological fix? Which is the more politically and socially acceptable? Which is more fun?
- What would it take to move mass cuisine in a more sustainable direction?

NOTES

Chapter 1 Why Study Food?

1. Parts of this essay are adapted from Belasco 1999 and Belasco 2002b.
2. This quotation is one of the dozen or so wise sayings chiseled into the interior dome of the Library of Congress' Main Reading Room.

Chapter 2 Identity: Are We What We Eat?

1. "Twist.Lick.Dunk.Oreo." See: http://eat-all-you-,want.blogspot.com/2006_05_01_eat-all-you-want_archive.html, accessed August 30, 2006; Also: "Superlaugh," http://www.superlaugh.com/1/oreo.htm, accessed August 30, 2006. "Oreo and Milk Memories," http://www.nabiscoworld.com/oreo/memories/, accessed August 30, 2006.
2. Adair Lara, "Ode to Oreos," *Cooking Light*, March/April 1993, 170.
3. These 500 anonymous memoirs were collected between 1990 and 2006.
4. It's hard to keep up with the world of corporate mega-mergers. Nabisco was founded in 1898 and was acquired by R. J. Reynolds Tobacco in 1985. Philip Morris (PM) bought Nabisco in 2000 and merged it into its Kraft Foods Division, which PM had acquired in 1988. PM renamed itself Altria in 2001 and then spun off Kraft – and Oreos – in 2007.
5. Walt Whitman, "Song of Myself," *Leaves of Grass*, 185–55.

Chapter 3 The Drama of Food: Divided Identities

1. http://en.wikipedia.org/wiki/Consuming_Passions, accessed August 30, 2006.
2. http://www.vdb.org/smackn.acgi$tapedetail?CONSUMINGP, accessed August 30, 2006.
3. The lyrics for all of the songs mentioned in this chapter are easily found on the Web.
4. Brita Belli, "A Little Latin Love," FairfieldWeekly.com, July 20, 2006, http://www.ctnow.com/custom/nmm/fairfieldweekly/hce-fcw-0720-ff30covintroconde30.artjul20,0,2645486.story, accessed August 31, 2006.
5. "Cow," Urban Dictionary, http://www.urbandictionary.com/define.php?term=cow, accessed August 31, 2006.
6. "Women farmers: influential players in the world of agriculture," International Federation of Agricultural Producers, October 15, 2004, http://www.ifap.org/news/press04.html, accessed July 31, 2007.
7. Karin Hamrick and Kristina Shelley, "How Much Time Do Americans Spend Preparing and Eating Food?" *AmberWaves*, November 2005, http://www.ers.usda.gov/AmberWaves/November05/DataFeature/, accessed July 31, 2007.
8. Museum of Burnt Food, http://www.burntfoodmuseum.com/#, accessed August 31, 2006.

9. Chris Rose, "Cooking Up Art – With her real meat bikini, performance artist makes a rare statement," *The Times-Picayune*, December 23, 2003, http://www.heatherweathers.com/TP_SMreview.html, accessed September 1, 2006; "JUDGE MEAT NOT WOMEN! Beauty Pageants A Bunch of Bologna!, http://www.nostatusquo.com/ACLU/Nikki/ann.html, accessed September 1, 2006; Vincent Canby, "Film: 'Gap-Toothed Women,' 'Miss … or Myth?'" *New York Times*, September 16, 1987, http://query.nytimes.com/gst/fullpage, accessed September 1, 2006.

Chapter 4   Convenience: The Global Food Chain

1. Ideas for using *Pancakes, Pancakes!* in the classroom, Official Eric Carle Website, accessed June 12, 2007, http://www.eric-carle.com/bb-pancake.html; Patricia King Robeson, "Economics and Geography Lessons: *Pancakes, Pancakes!*" accessed June 12, 2007, http://www.mcps.k12.md.us/curriculum/Socialstd/grade1/Pancakes.html.

2. McDonald's Breakfast Menu Extension, accessed June 12, 2007, http://www.petitiononline.com/lovinit/petition.html; John Schmeltzer, "McDonald's Says It's Up to Breakfast Challenges," *Chicago Tribune*, May 25, 2007, accessed June 12, 2007; http://www.chicagotribune.com/business/chi-fri_mcdonalds_5-24may25,1,1952503.story.

3. "Global Food Markets: Global Food Industry Structure," USDA, Economic Research Service, accessed June 11, 2007, http://www.ers.usda.gov/Briefing/GlobalFoodMarkets/Industry.htm; Anita Regmi and Mark Gehlhar, New Directions in Global Food Markets, USDA, Agriculture Information Bulletin No. (AIB794) 81 pp, February 2005, accessed June 11, 2007, http://www.ers.usda.gov/publications/aib794/.

4. Food Marketing Institute, SUPERMARKET FACTS Industry Overview 2006, accessed June 11, 2007, http://www.fmi.org/facts_figs/superfact.htm; "Introduction to the Food Industry," Plunkett Research, Ltd, accessed June 13, 2007, http://www.plunkettresearch.com/Industries/FoodBeverageTobacco/FoodBeverageTobaccoTrends/tabid/249/Default.aspx.

5. "Food Market Structures: Food Service," USDA, ERS, November 1, 2006; accessed June 11, 2007, http://www.ers.usda.gov/Briefing/FoodMarketStructures/foodservice.htm.

6. Schmeltzer, "McDonald's Says."

7. FAO Statistical Yearbook, 2005–06, accessed June 11, 2007, http://www.fao.org/es/ess/yearbook/vol_1_2/site_en.asp?page=cp.

8. US Farm and Farm-Related Employment, 2002, USDA, ERA, accessed June 11, 2007, http://www.ers.usda.gov/Data/FarmandRelatedEmployment/ViewData.asp?GeoAreaPick=STAUS_United+States&YearPick=2002&B1=Submit.

9. William Edmondson, "Food and Fiber System Important Part of Economy," *Rural America*, 17:1 (Spring 2002): 2. Accessed July 2, 2007, http://216.239.51.104/search?q=cache:rBc9BcpNWrwJ:www.ers.usda.gov/publications/ruralamerica/ra171/ra171g.pdf+food+and+fiber+system+employment&hl=en&ct=clnk&cd=1&gl=us.

10. FAO, Key Statistics of Food and Agricultural Trade for 2004, accessed June 11, 2007, http://www.fao.org/statistics/toptrade/trade.asp.

11. A "poke" is a small sack or bag (with the same origins as pocket). Thus to buy a pig that is hidden in a bag is to violate a basic rule of traditional shopping: buyer beware (*caveat emptor*), or make sure you can *see* what you're buying. According to medieval legend, the original con was to substitute a cat for a suckling pig in a sealed bag. To "let the cat out of the bag" was to reveal the scam.

12. "Food CPI, Prices and Expenditures: Food Expenditure Tables, USDA, ERS, accessed June 14, 2007, http://www.ers.usda.gov/Briefing/CPIFoodAndExpenditures/Data/.

13. "Introduction to the Food Industry," Plunkett Research, Ltd, accessed June 13, 2007, http://www.plunkettresearch.com/Industries/FoodBeverageTobacco/FoodBeverageTobaccoTrends/tabid/249/Default.aspx.

14. Sonu Jain, "India Losing Battle vs. Hunger," *Expressindia.Com*, October 14, 2006, accessed June 22, 2007, http://www.expressindia.com/fullstory.php?newsid=75521.

15. William Darby, "Fulfilling the Scientific Community's Responsibilities for Nutrition and Food Safety," *Food Technology*, 26:8, August 1972, 35.

16. What follows is adapted from Belasco 2006c.

17. For another example of how this analysis might be conducted for undergraduates, see Wilkins 2005.

18. "Sociology and the Global Politics of Food," St Cloud State University, accessed June 14, 2007, http://web.stcloudstate.edu/teore/Food/FoodPolitics.htm.

19. Highly recommended social histories of farming include: Goldschmidt (1978), Danbom (1995), Stoll (1998), Fite (1981). Also, for detailed research on the challenges faced by modern farms and their communities: *Agriculture and Human Values,* a quarterly journal published by the Agriculture, Food, and Human Values Association. http://www.afhvs.org/.

20. Other highly readable, informally ethnographic portraits of farmers: Horwitz (1998), Rhodes (1989), Hanson (1996), Kohn (1988).

21. For a complete, annotated bibliography of McPhee's works, see John McPhee Bookshelf, accessed June 14, 2007, http://www.johnmcphee.com/bookshelf.htm.

22. Margaret Webb Pressler, "New, Improved! So What." *Washington Post*, April 4, 2004, F5.

23. Mega Mac commercial, accessed June 20, 2007, http://www.japanprobe.com/?p=915; "Mega Mac to Go, Please," *Japan Today*, January 12, 2007, accessed June 20, 2007, http://www.japantoday.com/jp/product/1168.

Chapter 5   Responsibility: Who Pays for Dinner?

1. Eric Partridge, *Origins: A Short Etymological Dictionary of Modern English* (New York: Greenwich House, 1983), 149.

2. Robert Heinlein, *The Moon is a Harsh Mistress* (1966).

3. Taken from Belasco 2006c.

4. See Internet Sacred Text Archive, accessed June 25, 2007, http://www.sacred-texts.com/search.htm.

5. "Food Safety and Food-borne Illness," World Health Organization Fact Sheet no. 237, reviewed March 2007, accessed June 26, 2007, http://www.who.int/mediacentre/factsheets/fs237/en/; "Food-borne diseases, emerging," World Health Organization Fact Sheet no.124, revised January 2002, accessed June 26, 2007, http://www.who.int/mediacentre/factsheets/fs124/en/.

6. "Economics of Food-borne Disease," USDA, Economic Research Service, July 24, 2004, accessed June 26, 2007, http://www.ers.usda.gov/briefing/Food-borneDisease/.

7. Ahmed El Amin, "UK food-borne disease cases fall by 19 percent," Food Production Daily.Com, October 10, 2006, accessed June 26, 2007, http://foodproductiondaily.com/news/ng.asp?id=71164-fsa-food-borne-campylobacter.

8. "Food-borne disease," FAO/WHO Global Forum of Food Safety Regulators, Marrakech, Morocco, 28–30 January 2002, accessed June 26, 2007, http://www.fao.org/DOCREP/MEETING/004/AB524E.HTM#P60_9306.

9. "Travelers' Diarrhea," US Centers for Disease Control, accessed June 27, 2007, http://www.cdc.gov/ncidod/dbmd/diseaseinfo/travelersdiarrhea_g.htm.

10. Charles Dickens, *Little Dorrit*. Original 1857. New York: Modern Library, 2002: 107.

11. "Food-borne disease," FAO/WHO Global Forum of Food Safety Regulators, Marrakech, Morocco, 28–30 January 2002, accessed June 26, 2007, http://www.fao.org/DOCREP/MEETING/004/AB524E.HTM#P60_9306.

12. "Check Out That Restaurant," State of Alaska, Division of Environmental Health, Food Safety and Sanitation Program, accessed June 27, 2007, http://www.dec.state.ak.us/eh/fss/consumers/check_out_that_restaurant.htm.

13. "Deadly Habits," *Washington Post*, March 10, 2004, p.A1.

14. "Statistics Related to Overweight and Obesity," National Institute of Diabetes and Digestive and Kidney Diseases, US National Institutes of Health, updated October 2006, accessed June 28, 2007, http://win.niddk.nih.gov/statistics/index.htm#other.

15. "Obesity and Overweight," World Health Organization, 2003, accessed June 28, 2007, http://www.who.int/dietphysicalactivity/publications/facts/obesity/en/; Joan Ryan, "In Fat Race, US Leads, World Gains," *San Francisco Chronicle*, March 9, 2004, accessed June 28, 2007, http://sfgate.com/cgi-bin/article.cgi?f=/c/a/2004/03/09/BAGGU5GSR41.DTL; Elaine Sciolino, "France Battles a Problem that Grows and Grows: Fat," *New York Times*, January 25, 2006, accessed June 28, 2007; http://www.nytimes.com/2006/01/25/international/europe/25obese.html?ex=1183176000&en=a9b35194449ada84&ei=5070; "Obesity Rate Triples," BBC News, February 15, 2001, accessed June 28, 2007, http://newsvote.bbc.co.uk/1/hi/health/1170787.stm.

16. Rob Stein, "Obesity May Stall Trend of Increasing Longevity," *Washington Post*, March 17, 2005, A2.

17. "Shocking Statistics," Student Wellness, University of Colorado at Boulder, accessed June 29, 2007, http://www.colorado.edu/StudentGroups/wellness/NewSite/BdyImgShockingStats.html.

18. Pascale Harter, "Mauritania's 'wife-fattening' farm," BBC News, January 26, 2004, accessed June 29, 2007, http://news.bbc.co.uk/2/hi/africa/3429903.stm.

19. Marsha Laux, "Pastured Poultry Profile," Agricultural Marketing Resource Center, April 2007, accessed July 5, 2007, http://www.agmrc.org/agmrc/commodity/livestock/poultry/pasturedpoultryprofile.htm.

20. "McDonald's Says No More Playing Chicken with Antibiotics," *Environmental Defense*, June 17, 2003, accessed July 5, 2007, http://www.environmentaldefense.org/article.cfm?ContentID=2851; Marc Kaufman, "McDonald's Will Tell Meat Suppliers to Cut Antibiotics Use. Policy Reflects Concerns On Drug-Resistant Germs," *Washington Post*, June 19, 2003, page A03.

21. "Economically Active Population in Agriculture," *FAO Statistical Yearbook 2004–2005*, accessed July 2, 2007, http://www.fao.org/statistics/yearbook/vol_1_1/site_en.asp?page=resources.

22. Paul Spike, "How America Inspired the Third Reich," *The First Post*, May 31, 2007, accessed July 5, 2007, http://www.thefirstpost.co.uk/index.php?storyID=7083.

23. USDA Nutrient Data Laboratory: http://www.ars.usda.gov/main/site_main.htm?modecode=12354500.

Chapter 6   The Future of Food

1. Jonathan Swift, "A Voyage to Brobdingnag," *Gulliver's Travels,* part 2, pp. 119–20, in *The Prose Works of Jonathan Swift,* (ed.) Herbert Davis, Vol. 11 (1941).

2. World Population Information, US Census Bureau, accessed July 9, 2007, http://www.census.gov/ipc/www/world.html.

3. "Chinese Concern at Obesity Surge," BBC News, October 12, 2004, accessed August 3, 2007, http://news.bbc.co.uk/2/hi/asia-pacific/3737162.stm.

4. Jeff Cox, "Corn: The Inflation Crop," CNNMoney.com, March 28, 2007, accessed August 3, 2007, http://money.cnn.com/2007/03/27/news/economy/corn_prices/index.htm.

5. "The 2,400-Liter Hamburger," Private Sector Development Blog, World Bank Group, April 16, 2007, accessed July 10, 2007, http://psdblog.worldbank.org/psdblog/water_and_sanitation/.

6. Paul G. Townsley, "Western Water in the Age of Scarcity," Western Conference of Public Service Commissioners, June 12, 2007, Park City, Utah, accessed July 10, 2007, http://216.239.51.104/search?q=cache:SMWRL0kPeDsJ:www.psc.state.ut.us/WCPSC%2520Conference%25202007/Speaker%2520Presentations/Western%2520PSC%2520Conference%2520-%2520Comments%2520of%2520Paul%2520G%2520Townsley.doc+colorado+river+water+scarcity&hl=en&ct=clnk&cd=6&gl=us.

7. One hectare is 10,000 square meters, or about 2.5 acres.

8. "Losing Soil and Fertility," Earth Policy Institute, 2005, accessed July 13, 2007, http://www.earth-policy.org/Books/Out/Ote5_2.htm.

9. "Losing Soil and Fertility," Earth Policy Institute, 2005, accessed July 13, 2007, http://www.earth-policy.org/Books/Out/Ote5_2.htm

10. For a recent overview of the technological fix, see Rosner 2004.

11. See also Conway 1997.

12. I first learned of this concept in Gussow 1978: 56, who attributes it to international law professor Richard Falk, "The Wrong Species for Nuclear Power," *Business and Society Review* (Fall 1976): 40–42.

BIBLIOGRAPHY

Abarca, Meredith E. (2001), "*Los Chilaquiles de mi 'ama*': The Language of Everyday Cooking," in Sherrie A. Inness (ed.), *Pilaf, Pozole, and Pad Thai: American Women and Ethnic Food*, Amherst, MA: University of Massachusetts Press, pp. 119–44.

Abu-Jaber, Diana (2005), *The Language of Baklava: A Memoir*, New York: Anchor.

Adams, Carol J. (1992), *The Sexual Politics of Meat: A Feminist-Vegetarian Critical Theory*, New York: Continuum.

Adler, Elizabeth (1983), "Creative Eating: The Oreo Syndrome," in Michael Owen Jones (ed.), "*Foodways and Eating Habits: Directions for Research*, California: California Folklore Society, pp. 4–10.

Albala, Ken (2007), *The Banquet: Dining in the Great Courts of Late Renaissance Europe*, Urbana: University of Illinois.

Allen, Gary (2000), "Desire on the Menu," *Journal for the Study of Food and Society* 4(2): 29–38.

Allison, Anne (1997), "Japanese Mothers and Obentos: The Lunch Box as Ideological State Apparatus," in Carole M. Counihan and Penny Van Esterik (eds), *Food and Culture: A Reader*, New York: Routledge, pp. 296–315.

Amato, Joseph (2000), *Dust: A History of the Small and Invisible*, Berkeley: University of California Press.

Appadurai, Arjun (1981), "GastroPolitics in Hindu South Asia," *American Ethnologist* 8(3): 494–511.

Avakian, Arlene Voski (ed.) (1997), *Through the Kitchen Window: Women Writers Explore the Intimate Meanings of Food and Cooking*, Boston: Beacon Press.

Avakian, Arlene Voski and Haber, Barbara (eds) (2005), *From Betty Crocker to Feminist Food Studies: Critical Perspectives on Women and Food*, Amherst, MA: University of Massachusetts Press.

Barling, David (2004). "Food Agencies as an Institutional Response to Policy Failure by the UK and the EU," in Mark Harvey, Andrew McKeekin and Alan Warde (eds), *Qualities of Food*, Manchester: Manchester University Press, pp. 108–28.

Barndt, Deborah (2002), *Tangled Routes: Women, Work, and Globalization on the Tomato Trail*, Lanham, MD: Rowman & Littlefield.

Baron, Cynthia (2006), "Dinner and a Movie: Analyzing Food and Film," *Food, Culture and Society* 9(1): 93–117.

Barthes, Roland (1979), "Toward a Psychosociology of Food Consumption," in Robert Forster and Orest Ranum (eds), *Food and Drink in History*, Baltimore, MD: Johns Hopkins University Press, pp. 166–73.

Belasco, Warren (1979), "Toward a Culinary Common Denominator: The Rise of Howard Johnson's, 1925–1940," *Journal of American Culture* 2(3): 503–18.

Belasco, Warren (1987), "Ethnic Fast Foods: The Corporate Melting Pot," *Food and Foodways* 2: 1–30.

Belasco, Warren (1999), "Why Food Matters," *Culture and Agriculture* 21(Spring): 27–34.

Belasco, Warren (2001), "Fast Food" in Jay Mechling (ed.), *Encyclopedia of American Studies*, New York: Grolier.

Belasco, Warren and Scranton, Philip (eds) (2002a), *Food Nations: Selling Taste in Consumer Societies*, New York: Routledge.

Belasco, Warren (2002b), "Food Matters: Perspectives on an Emerging Field," in Warren Belasco and Philip Scranton (eds), *Food Nations: Selling Taste in Consumer Societies*, New York: Routledge, pp. 2–23.

Belasco, Warren (2006a), *Meals to Come: A History of the Future of Food*, Berkeley: University of California Press.

Belasco, Warren (2006b), *Appetite for Change: How the Counterculture Took on the Food Industry*, Second updated edition, Ithaca, NY: Cornell University Press.

Belasco, Warren (2006c), "How Much Depends on Dinner?" Keynote address, conference on "Food Chains: Provisioning, Technology, and Science," Hagley Museum and Library, Wilmington, DE, November 3, 2006.

Bentley, Amy (1998), *Eating for Victory: Food Rationing and the Politics of Domesticity*, Urbana: University of Illinois Press.

Berquist, Kathleen Ja Sook (2006), "From Kim Chee to Moon Cakes: Feeding Asian Adoptees' Imaginings of Culture and Self," *Food, Culture and Society* 9(2): 141–54.

Berry, Wendell (1970), *A Continuous Harmony: Essays Cultural and Agricultural*, New York: Harcourt Brace Jovanovich.

Berry, Wendell (1989), "The Pleasures of Eating," *Journal of Gastronomy* 5(2): 125–31.

Bestor, Theodore C. (2004), *Tsukiji: The Fish Market at the Center of the World*, Berkeley: University of California Press.

Bonnano, Allesandro, Busch, Lawrence, Friedland, William, Gouveia, Lourdes and Mingione, Enzo (1994), *From Columbus to ConAgra: The Globalization of Agriculture and Food*, Lawrence, KS: University of Kansas Press.

Boorstin, Sharon (2002), *Let Us Eat Cake: Adventures in Food and Friendship*, New York: Regan Books.

Borrero, Mauricio (2002), "Food and the Politics of Scarcity in Urban Soviet Russia, 1917–1941," in Warren Belasco and Philip Scranton (eds), *Food Nations: Selling Taste in Consumer Societies*, New York: Routledge, pp. 258–76.

Bower, Anne L. (ed.) (1997), *Recipes for Reading: Community Cookbooks, Stories, Histories*, Amherst, MA: University of Massachusetts Press.

Bower, Anne L. (ed.) (2004), *Reel Food: Essays on Food and Film*, New York: Routledge.

Brembeck, Helene (2005), "Home to McDonald's: Upholding the Family Dinner with the Help of McDonald's," *Food, Culture and Society* 8(2): 215–26.

Brewster, Leitita, and Michael Jacobson (1983), *The Changing American Diet: A Chronicle of American Eating Habits from 1910–1980*, Washington, DC: Center for Science in the Public Interest.

Brittain, Robert (1952), *Let There Be Bread*, New York: Simon & Schuster.

Brown, Lester (1995), *Who Will Feed China? Wake-Up Call for a Small Planet*, New York: Norton.

Brown, Linda Keller and Mussell, Kay (eds), *Ethnic and Regional Foodways in the United States: The Performance of Group Identity*, Knoxville: University of Tennessee Press.

Brown, Marcia (1947), *Stone Soup*, New York: Atheneum.

Brownell, Kelly D. and Horgen, Katherine Battle (2004), *Food Fight: The Inside Story of the Food Industry, America's Obesity Crisis, and What We Can Do About It*, Chicago: Contemporary Books.

Brumberg, Joan Jacobs (1989), *Fasting Girls: The History of Anorexia Nervosa*, New York: Plume.

Byrnes, J. (1976), "Raising Pigs by the Calendar at Maplewood Farm," *Hog Farm Management* (September): 30.

Caldwell, Melissa L. (2005), "Domesticating the French Fry: McDonald's and Consumerism in Moscow," in James L. Watson and Melissa L. Caldwell (eds), *The Cultural Politics of Eating: A Reader*, Oxford: Blackwell and Caldwell (2005), pp. 180–96.

Callenbach, Ernest (1975), *Ecotopia*. New York: Bantam Books.

Campos, Paul (2004), *The Obesity Myth: Why America's Obsession with Weight is Hazardous to Your Health*, New York: Gotham.

Carle, Eric (1990), *Pancakes, Pancakes!*, New York: Simon & Schuster.

Charles, Daniel (2001), *Lords of the Harvest: Biotech, Big Money, and the Future of Food*, Cambridge, MA: Perseus Publishing.

Carlin, Joseph M. (2004), "Saloons," in Andrew F. Smith (ed.), *The Oxford Encyclopedia of Food and Drink in America*, New York: Oxford University Press, pp. 387–89.

Cole, James (2006), "Consuming Passions: Reviewing the Evidence for Cannibalism within the Prehistoric Archeological Record," *Assemblage* 9 (June), http://www.assemblage.group. shef.ac.uk/issue9/cole.html, accessed April 8, 2008.

Commoner, Barry (1971), *The Closing Circle*, New York: Knopf.

Conway, Gordon (1997), *The Doubly Green Revolution: Food for All in the Twenty-First Century*, Ithaca, NY: Cornell University Press.

Counihan, Carole M. (2004), *Around the Tuscan Table: Food, Family, and Gender in Twentieth-Century Florence*, New York: Routledge.

Counihan, Carole M. and Van Esterik, Penny (eds) (1997), *Food and Culture: A Reader*, New York: Routledge.

Coveney, John (2006), *Food, Morals and Meaning: The Pleasure and Anxiety of Eating*, London: Routledge.

Cowan, Ruth Schwartz (1983), *More Work for Mother: The Ironies of Household Technology from the Open Hearth to the Microwave*, New York: Basic Books.

Critser, Greg (2003), *Fat Land: How Americans Became the Fattest People in the World*, New York: Houghton Mifflin.

Cronon, William (1983), *Changes in the Land: Indians, Colonists, and the Ecology of New England*, New York: Hill and Wang.

Cronon, William (1991), *Nature's Metropolis: Chicago and the Great West*, New York: Norton.

Curtin, Deane and Heldke, Lisa M. (eds) (1992), *Cooking, Eating, and Thinking: Transformative Philosophies of Food*, Bloomington, IN: Indiana University Press.

Dalby, Andrew (2000), *Dangerous Tastes: The Story of Spices*, Berkeley: University of California Press.

Dalton, Sharron (2004), *Our Overweight Children: What Parents, Schools, and Communities Can Do to Control the Fatness Epidemic*, Berkeley: University of California Press.

Dam, Henry J. W. (1894), "Foods in the Year 2000," *McLure's Magazine* (September): 303–12.

Danbom, David B. (1995), *Born in the Country: A History of Rural America*, Baltimore, MD: Johns Hopkins University Press.

Davidson, James (1999), *Courtesans and Fishcakes: The Consuming Passions of Classical Athens*, New York: Harper Perennial.

De Silva, Cara (ed.) (1996), *In Memory's Kitchen: A Legacy from the Women of Terezin*, Northvale, NJ: Jason Aronson Inc.

Devall, Bill (1988), *Simple in Means, Rich in Ends: Practicing Deep Ecology*, Salt Lake City: Peregrine Smith Press.

DeVault, Marjorie L. (1991), *Feeding the Family: The Social Organization of Caring as Gendered Work*, Chicago: University of Chicago Press.

Diamond, Jared (1999), *Guns, Germs, and Steel: The Fates of Human Societies*, New York: Norton.

Dietler, Michael and Hayden, Brian (eds) (2001), *Feasts: Archeological and Ethnographic Perspectives on Food, Politics, and Power*, Washington, DC: Smithsonian Institution Press.

Dietz, William (2005), "Overview of the Obesity Epidemic," paper prepared for an expert panel on "Exploring a Multi-Disciplinary Approach to Overweight and Obesity in the United States," Centers for Disease Control, Washington, DC, September 7–8, 2005.

Diner, Hasia (2001), *Hungering for America: Italian, Irish, and Jewish Foodways in the Age of Migration*, Cambridge, MA: Harvard University Press.

Dixon, Jane and Broom, Dorothy H. (eds) (2007), *The Seven Deadly Sins of Obesity: How the Modern World is Making Us Fat*, Sydney: UNSW Press.

Douglas, Mary (1975), "Deciphering a Meal," in Carole M. Counihan and Penny Van Esterik (eds), *Food and Culture: A Reader*, New York: Routledge, pp. 36–54.

Drewnowski, Adam (1999), "Fat and Sugar in the Global Diet: Dietary Diversity in the Nutrition Transition," in Raymond Grew (ed.), *Food in Global History*, Boulder, CO: Westview, pp. 194–206.

Dufresne, John (1998), "Nothing to Eat but Food: Menu as Memoir," in Mark Winegardner (ed.), *We Are What We Ate: Twenty-Four Memories of Food*, New York: Harcourt Brace & Co., pp. 80–92.

East, Edward M. (1924), *Mankind at the Crossroads*, New York: Charles Scribner's Sons.

Egerton, March (ed.) (1994), *Since Eve Ate Apples*, Portland, OR: Tsunami Press.

Ehrman, Edwina, Forsyth, Hazel, Peltz, Lucy and Ross, Cathy (1999), *London Eats Out: 500 Years of Capital Dining*, London: Philip Wilson.

Ettlinger, Steve (2007), *Twinkie, Deconstructed*, New York: Hudson Street Press.

Etzioni, Amitai (ed.) (2004), *We Are What We Celebrate: Understanding Holidays and Rituals*, New York: New York University Press.

Farb, Peter and Armelagos, George (1980), *Consuming Passions: The Anthropology of Eating*, Boston: Houghton Mifflin.

Fiddes, Nick (1991), *Meat: A Natural Symbol*, London: Routledge.

Fine, Gary Alan (1996), *Kitchens: The Culture of Restaurant Work*, Berkeley: University of California Press.

Finkelstein, Eric A., Fiebelkorn, Ian C. and Wang, Guijing (2003), "National Medical Spending Attributable To Overweight And Obesity: How Much, And Who's Paying?" *Health Affairs*, May 14, accessed June 28, 2007, http://content.healthaffairs.org/cgi/content/full/hlthaff.w3.219v1/DC1.

Finn, John E. (2004), "The Kitchen Voice as Confessional," *Food, Culture and Society* 7(1): 85–100.

Fischler, Claude (1999), "The 'Mad Cow' Crisis: A Global Perspective," in Raymond Grew (ed.), *Food in Global History*, Boulder, CO: Westview, pp. 207–13.

Fite, Gilbert C. (1981), *American Farmers: The New Minority*, Bloomington: Indiana University Press.

Fitzpatrick, Joan (2007), *Food in Shakespeare: Early Modern Dietaries and the Play*, Aldershot: Ashgate.

Flanders, Judith (2006), *Consuming Passions: Leisure and Pleasure in Victorian Britain*, New York: Harper.

Foster, John Bellamy and Magdoff, Fred (2000), "Liebig, Marx, and the Depletion of Soil Fertility: Relevance for Today's Agriculture," in Fred Magdoff, John Bellamy Foster and Frederick H. Buttel (eds), *Hungry for Profit: The Agribusiness Threat to Farmers, Food, and the Environment*, New York: Monthly Review Press, pp. 43–60.

Fowler, Cary and Mooney, Pat (1990), *Shattering: Food Politics, and the Loss of Genetic Diversity*, Tucson, AZ: University of Arizona Press.

Fox, Nicols (1997), *Spoiled: Why Our Food is Making Us Sick, and What We Can Do About It*, New York: Penguin.

Fraser, Laura (1997), *Losing It: False Hopes and Fat Profits in the Diet Industry*, New York: Plume.

Friedensohn, Doris (2006), *Eating as I Go: Scenes from America and Abroad*, Lexington: University Press of Kentucky.

Fromartz, Samuel (2006), *Organic Inc.: Natural Foods and How They Grew*, New York: Harcourt.

Fuller, Frank and Hayes, Dermot J. (1998), "The Impact of Chinese Accession to the World Trade Organization on US Meat and Feed-Grain Producers," Center for Agricultural and Rural Development, Iowa State University, Working Paper 98-WP195, July. Accessed July 10, 2007, http://216.239.51.104/search?q=cache:0A6EpuCXWN0J:www.card.iastate. edu/publications/DBS/PDFFiles/98wp195.pdf+egg+grain+conversion+ratio&hl=en&ct= clnk&cd=15&gl=us.

Gabaccia, Donna (1998), *We Are What We Eat: Ethnic Foods and the Making of Americans*, Cambridge, MA: Harvard University Press.

Gard, Michael, and Jan Wright (2005), *The Obesity Epidemic: Science, Morality and Ideology*, London: Routledge.

Gardner, Gary (1996), *Shrinking Fields: Cropland Loss in a World of Eight Billion*, Worldwatch Paper 131, Washington, DC: Worldwatch Institute.

George, Kathryn Paxton (1994), "Should Feminists Be Vegetarians?" *Signs* 19(Winter): 405–34.

Germov, John and Williams, Lauren (eds) (1999), *The Social Appetite: A Sociology of Nutrition*, Oxford: Oxford University Press.

Giedion, Siegfried (1979) [1948], *Mechanization Takes Command: A Contribution to Anonymous History*, New York: Norton.

Gilman, Charlotte Perkins (1966) [1898], *Women and Economics: The Economic Factor between Men and Women as a Factor in Social Evolution*, New York: Harper Torchbooks.

Gilman, Charlotte Perkins (1970) [1915], *Herland*, New York: Pantheon Books.

Gilman, Charlotte Perkins (1972) [1903], *The Home: Its Work and Influence*, Urbana IL: University of Illinois Press.

Goldschmidt, Walter (1978), *As You Sow: Three Studies in the Social Consequences of Agribusiness* (update of original 1947 ed.), Montclair, NJ: Allanheld, Osmun and Co.

Goudie, Andrew (1990), *The Human Impact on the Natural Environment*, third ed. Cambridge, MA: MIT Press.

Green, Harvey and Perry, Mary-Ellen (2003), *The Light of the Home: An Intimate View of the Lives of Women in Victorian America*, Fayetteville: University of Arkansas Press.

Grew, Raymond (ed.) (1999), *Food in Global History*, Boulder, CO: Westview.

Griffiths, Siân and Wallace, Jennifer (eds) (1998), *Consuming Passions: Food in the Age of Anxiety*, Manchester: Manchester University Press.

Grover, Kathryn (ed.) (1987), *Dining in America, 1850–1900*, Amherst, MA: University of Massachusetts Press.

Guerron-Montero, Carla (2004), "Afro-Antillean Cuisine and Global Tourism," *Food, Culture and Society* 7(2): 29–48.

Gussow, Joan Dye (ed.) (1978), *The Feeding Web: Issues in Nutritional Ecology*, Palo Alto, CA: Bull Publishing.

Gussow, Joan Dye (2001), *This Organic Life*, White River Junction, VT: Chelsea Green.

Guy, Kolleen M. (2002), "Rituals of Pleasure in the Land of Treasures: Wine Consumption and the Making of French Identity in the Late Nineteenth Century," in Warren Belasco and Philip Scranton (eds), *Food Nations: Selling Taste in Consumer Societies*, New York: Routledge, pp. 34–47.

Haber, Barbara (2004), "Lydia Maria Child," in Andrew Smith (ed.), *The Oxford Encyclopedia of Food and Drink in America*, New York: Oxford University Press, p. 230.

Halter, Marilyn (2000), *Shopping for Identity: The Marketing of Ethnicity*, New York: Schocken Books.

Halweil, Brian (2004), *Eat Here: Reclaiming Homegrown Pleasures in a Global Supermarket*, New York: Norton.

Halweil, Brian (2006), "Grain Harvest Flat," *Vital Signs 2006–2007*, New York: Norton, pp. 22–3.

Hanson, Victor Davis (1996), *Fields without Dreams: Defending the Agrarian Idea*, New York: Free Press.

Hardin, Garrett (1993), *Living within Limits: Ecology, Economics, and Population Taboos*, New York: Oxford University Press.

Hauck-Lawson, Annie (1992), "Hearing the Food Voice: An Epiphany for a Researcher," *Digest* 12(1–2): 26–7.

Hauck-Lawson, Annie (2004), "Introduction to Special Issue on the Food Voice," *Food, Culture and Society* 7(1): 24–5.

Haverluk, Terrence W. (2002), "Chile Peppers and Identity Construction in Pueblo, Colorado," *Journal for the Study of Food and Society* 6(1): 45–59.

Heinzerling, Lisa, and Frank Ackerman (2002), *Pricing the Priceless: Cost-Benefit Analysis of Environmental Protection*, Washington, DC: Georgetown University Law Center, accessed June 27, 2007 at http://ase.tufts.edu/gdae/publications/C-B%20pamphlet%20final.pdf.

Heldke, Lisa (2003), *Exotic Appetites: Ruminations of a Food Adventurer*, New York: Routledge.

Heldke, Lisa (2006), "The Unexamined Meal is Not Worth Eating, Or Why and How Philosophers (Might/Could/Do) Study Food," *Food, Culture and Society* 9(2): 201–19.

Hilberg, Raul (1961) *The Destruction of the European Jews*, Chicago, IL: Quadrangle.

Hirshorn, Paul, and Steven Izenour (1979), *White Tower*, Cambridge, MA: MIT Press.

Hoffmann, Sandra A. and Taylor, Michael R. (eds) (2005), *Toward Safer Food: Perspectives on Risk and Priority Setting*, Washington, DC: Resources for the Future.

Horowitz, Roger (2006), *Putting Meat on the American Table: Taste, Technology, Transformation*, Baltimore, MD: Johns Hopkins University Press.

Horwitz, Richard P. (1998), *Hog Ties: Pigs, Manure, and Mortality in American Culture*, New York: St Martin's Press.

Hunter, Emily (2006), "Selling Out: The Ben 'n' Jerry's Story," American Studies Senior Seminar Paper, University of Maryland, Baltimore County.

Inness, Sherrie A. (ed.) (2001a), *Kitchen Culture in America: Popular Representations of Food, Gender and Race*, Philadelphia: University of Pennsylvania.

Inness, Sherrie (2001b), *Dinner Roles: American Women and Culinary Culture*, Iowa City: University of Iowa Press.

Jackson, Wes, Berry, Wendell and Colman, Bruce (eds) (1994), *Meeting the Expectations of the Land: Essays in Sustainable Agriculture and Stewardship*, San Francisco: North Point Press.

Jacobs, Marc and Scholliers, Peter (eds) (2003), *Eating Out in Europe*, Oxford: Berg.

Jaine, Tom (1999), "Bread," in Alan Davidson (ed.), *Oxford Companion to Food*, New York: Oxford University Press, pp. 95–8.

Jansen, Sharon L. (1997), "'Family Liked 1956': My Mother's Recipes," in Arlene Voski Avakian (ed.), *Through the Kitchen Window: Women Writers Explore the Intimate Meanings of Food and Cooking*, Boston: Beacon Press, pp. 55–64.

Jenkins, Virginia Scott (2000), *Bananas: An American History*, Washington, DC: Smithsonian Institution Press.

Julier, Alice (2004), "Entangled in Our Meals: Guilt and Pleasure in Contemporary Food Discourses," *Food, Culture and Society* 7(1): 13–21.

Kaufman, Cathy K. (2004), "Sauces and Gravies," in Andrew Smith (ed.), *The Oxford Encyclopedia of Food and Drink in America II*, New York: Oxford University Press, pp. 403–7.

Kempf, Stephanie (1997), *Finding Solutions of Hunger: Kids Can Make a Difference*, New York: World Hunger Year.

Kevles, Daniel (1985), *In the Name of Eugenics: Genetics and the Uses of Human Heredity*, New York: Knopf.

Kingsolver, Barbara (2007), *Animal, Vegetable, Miracle: A Year of Food Life*, New York: HarperCollins.

Kneen, Brewster (1999), *Farmageddon: Food and the Culture of Biotechnology*, Gabriola Island, BC: New Society Publishers.

Kohn, Howard (1988), *The Last Farmer: An American Memoir*, New York: Summit Books.

Korsmeyer, Carolyn (1991), *Making Sense of Taste: Food and Philosophy*, Ithaca, NY: Cornell University Press.

Kulick, Don and Meneley, Anne (eds) (2005), *Fat: The Anthropology of an Obsession*, New York: Tarcher/Penguin.

Kumin, Beat (2003), "Eating Out before the Restaurant: Dining Cultures in Early Modern Inns," in Marc Jacobs and Peter Scholliers (eds), *Eating Out in Europe*, Oxford: Berg, pp. 71–88.

Kurlansky, Mark (1997), *Cod*, New York: Knopf.

Kurlansky, Mark (2002), *Salt: A World History*, New York: Walker and Company.

Kurlansky, Mark (2006), *The Big Oyster: History on the Half Shell*, New York: Ballantine.

Lane, Mary E. Bradley (1975) [1880], *Mizora: A Prophecy*, Boston: Gregg Press.

Lappé, Frances Moore (1971), *Diet for a Small Planet*, New York: Ballantine.

Lappé, Frances Moore (1982), *Diet for a Small Planet: Tenth Anniversary Edition*, New York: Ballantine.

Lappé, Frances Moore, Collins, Joseph, Rosset, Peter and Esparza, Luis (1998), *World Hunger: Twelve Myths*, 2nd edn, New York: Grove Press.

Lara, Adair (1993), "Ode to Oreos," *Cooking Light* (March/April): 170.

Laudan, Rachel (1996), *The Food of Paradise. Exploring Hawaii's Culinary Heritage*, Honolulu: University of Hawaii Press.

Laudan, Rachel (2001), "A Plea for Culinary Modernism: Why We Should Love New, Fast, Processed Food," *Gastronomica* 1:1 (February 2001): 36–44.

Lentz, Carola (ed.) (1999), *Changing Food Habits: Case Studies from Africa, South America, and Europe*, Amsterdam: Harwood.

Levenstein, Harvey (1988), *Revolution at the Table: The Transformation of the American Diet*, New York: Oxford University Press.

Levenstein, Harvey (1993), *Paradox of Plenty: A Social History of Eating in Modern America*, New York: Oxford University Press.

Lien, Marianne Elisabeth and Nerlich, Brigitte (eds) (2005), *The Politics of Food*, Oxford: Berg Publishers.

Logsdon, Gene (1994), *At Nature's Pace: Farming and the American Dream*, New York: Pantheon Books.

Long, Lucy M. (ed.) (2003), *Culinary Tourism*, Lexington: University Press of Kentucky.

Lovenheim, Peter (2002), *Portrait of a Burger as Young Calf: The Story of One Man, Two Cows, and the Feeding of a Nation*, New York: Three Rivers Press.

Mack, Arien (ed.) (1999), "Food: Nature and Culture," *Social Research* 66(1).

Madden, Etta M. and Finch, Martha L. (eds) (2006), *Eating in Eden: Food and American Utopias*, Lincoln: University of Nebraska Press.

Magdoff, Fred, Foster, John Bellamy and Buttel, Frederick H. (eds) (2000), *Hungry for Profit: The Agribusiness Threat to Farmers, Food, and the Environment*, New York: Monthly Review Press.

Malthus, Thomas (1985) [1798], *An Essay on the Principle of Population*, London: Penguin.

Manuel, Frank E. (1965), *The Prophets of Paris*, New York: Harper Torchbooks.

Marcus, Eric (2005), *Meat Market: Animals, Ethics, and Money*, New York: Brio.

Mason, Jim, and Singer, Peter (1990), *Animal Factories: What Agribusiness is Doing to the Family Farm, the Environment, and Your Health*, Revised and Updated Edition, New York: Harmony Books.

Matejowsky, Ty (2007), "SPAM and Fast Food 'Glocalization' in the Philippines," *Food, Culture and Society* 10(1): 23–41.

Mather, Robin (1996), *A Garden of Unearthly Delights: Bioengineering and the Future of Food*, New York: Plume.

Maurer, Donna (2002), *Vegetarianism: Movement or Moment?* Philadelphia: Temple University Press.

Mayo, Amanda (2007), "Can Commensal Eating be Eating Alone?" Paper at the annual meeting of the Association for the Study of Food and Society, Victoria BC, May 31.

McLean, Alice (2004), "Tasting Language: The Aesthetic Pleasures of Elizabeth David," *Food, Culture and Society* 7(1): 37–46.

McMichael, Philip (ed.) (1994), *The Global Restructuring of Agro-Food Systems*, Ithaca, NY: Cornell University Press.

McMillen, Wheeler (1929), *Too Many Farmers: The Story of What is Here and Ahead in Agriculture*, New York: William Morrow.

McPhee, John (1971), *Encounters with the Archdruid: Narratives about a Conservationist and Three of His Natural Enemies*, New York: Farrar, Straus & Giroux.

McWilliams, James E. (2005), *A Revolution in Eating: How the Quest for Food Shapes America*, New York: Columbia University Press.

Meadows, Donella H., Meadows, Dennis L. and Randers, Jorgen (1992), *Beyond the Limits: Global Collapse or a Sustainable Future*, London: Earthscan Publications.

Mennell, Stephen, Murcott, Anne and van Otterloo, Anneke (1992), *The Sociology of Food: Eating, Diet, and Culture*, London: Sage.

Mennell, Stephen (1996), *All Manners of Food: Eating and Taste in England and France from the Middle Ages to the Present*, 2nd edn, Urbana, IL: University of Illinois Press.

Menzel, Peter and D'Aluisio, Faith (2005), *Hungry Planet*, Berkeley: Ten Speed Press.

Merchant, Carolyn (1989), *Ecological Revolutions: Nature, Gender, and Science in New England*, Chapel Hill, NC: University of North Carolina Press.

Mintz, Sidney (1986), *Sweetness and Power: The Place of Sugar in Modern History*, New York: Penguin.

Mintz, Sidney (1996), "Eating American," in *Tasting Food, Tasting Freedom: Excursions into Eating, Culture, and the Past*, Boston: Beacon Press, pp. 106–24.

Mokeddem, Malika (2000), *Of Dreams and Assassins*, Charlottesville, VA: University of Virginia Press.

Montanari, Massimo (1999), "Food Systems and Models of Civilization," in Jean-Louis Flandrin and Massimo Montanari (eds), *Food: A Culinary History from Antiquity to the Present*, New York: Columbia University Press, pp. 69–78.

Morton, Timothy (ed.) (2004), *Cultures of Taste/ Theories of Appetite: Eating Romanticism*, New York: Palgrave Macmillan.

Murcott, Anne (1983), "'It's a Pleasure to Cook for Him': Food, Mealtimes and Gender in Some South Wales Households," in E. Gamarnikow et al. (eds), *The Public and the Private*, London: Heinemann, pp. 78–90.

Murray, Douglas L. (1994), *Cultivating Crisis: The Human Costs of Pesticides in Latin America*, Austin: University of Texas Press.

Nabhan, Gary Paul (1989), *Enduring Seeds: Native American Agriculture and Wild Plant Conservation*, San Francisco: North Point Press.

Nasser, Mervat (1997), *Culture and Weight Consciousness*, London: Routledge.

Nestle, Marion (2003), *Safe Food: Bacteria, Biotechnology, and Bioterrorism*, Berkeley: University of California Press.

Neuhaus, Jessamyn (2003), *Manly Meals and Mom's Home Cooking: Cookbooks and Gender in Modern America*, Baltimore, MD: Johns Hopkins University Press.

Newman, Leslea (1995), *Eating Our Hearts Out: Personal Accounts of Women's Relationship to Food*, Freedom, CA: The Crossing Press.

Nierenberg, Danielle (2005), *Happier Meals: Rethinking the Global Meat Industry*, Worldwatch Paper 171, Washington, DC: Worldwatch Institute.

Nierenberg, Danielle (2006), "Meat Consumption and Output Up," in *Vital Signs: 2006–2007*, New York: Norton, pp. 24–5.

Nissenbaum, Stephen (1988), *Sex, Diet and Debility in Jacksonian America: Sylvester Graham and Health Reform*, Chicago: Dorsey Press.

Oates, Joyce Carol (1993), "Food Mysteries," in Daniel Halpern (ed.), *Not for Bread Alone*, Hopewell, NJ: Ecco Press, pp. 25–37.

Orbach, Susie (2006) [1978], *Fat is a Feminist Issue*, New York: Arrow.

Orr, David (1994), *Earth in Mind: On Education, Environment, and the Human Prospect*, Washington, DC: Island Press.

Ozeki, Ruth L. (1999), *My Year of Meats*, New York: Penguin.

Parasecoli, Fabio (2004), "Food and Popular Culture: Teaching Critical Theory Through Food," *Food, Culture and Society* 7(1): 147–57.

Pelto, Gretel H. and Pelto, Pertti J. (1983), "Diet and Delocalization: Dietary Changes Since 1750," in Robert I. Rotberg and Theodore K. Rabb (eds), *Hunger and History: The Impact of Changing Food Production and Consumption Patterns on Society*, Cambridge: Cambridge University Press, pp. 309–30.

Pendergrast, Mark (1999), *Uncommon Grounds: The History of Coffee and How It Transformed Our World*, New York: Basic Books.

Pendergrast, Mark (2000), *For God, Country, and Coca-Cola*, 2nd edn, New York: Basic Books.

Penfold, Steve (2002), "'Eddie Shack Was No Tim Horton': Donuts and the Folklore of Mass Culture in Canada," in Warren Belasco and Philip Scranton (eds), *Food Nations: Selling Taste in Consumer Societies*, New York: Routledge, pp. 48–66.

Petrini, Carlo (2001), *Slow Food: The Case for Taste*, New York: Columbia University Press.

Piercy, Marge (1976), *Woman on the Edge of Time*, New York: Fawcett Crest.

Pilcher, Jeffrey M. (1998), *Que Vivan los Tamales! Food and the Making of Mexican Identity*, Albuquerque, NM: University of New Mexico Press.

Pilcher, Jeffrey M. (2006a), *The Sausage Rebellion: Public Health, Private Enterprise, and Meat in Mexico City, 1890–1917*, Albuquerque, NM: University of New Mexico Press.

Pilcher, Jeffrey M. (2006b), *Food in World History*, New York: Routledge.

Pillsbury, Richard (1998), *No Foreign Food: The American Diet in Time and Place*, Boulder, CO: Westview Press.

Pimentel, David, and Pimentel, Marcia (2004), "Land, Energy and Water Versus the Ideal US Population," Negative Population Growth Forum, accessed July 10, 2007, http://www.npg.org/forum_series/forum0205.html.

Pitts, Martin, Dorling, Danny and Pattie, Charles (2007), "Christmas Feasting and Social Class," *Food, Culture and Society* 10(3): 407–24.

Pleij, Herman (2001), *Dreaming of Cockaigne: Medieval Fantasies of the Perfect Life*, New York: Columbia University Press.

Pollan, Michael (2006), *The Omnivore's Dilemma: A Natural History of Four Meals*, New York: Penguin.

Popenoe, Rebecca (2005), "Ideal," in Don Kulick and Anne Meneley (eds), *Fat: The Anthropology of an Obsession*, New York: Tarcher/Penguin, pp. 9–28.

Poppendieck, Janet (1998), *Sweet Charity? Emergency Food and the End of Entitlement*, New York: Penguin.

Postel, Sandra (1996), *Dividing the Waters: Food Security, Ecosystem Health, and the New Politics of Scarcity*, Worldwatch Paper 132, Washington, DC: Worldwatch Institute.

Postel, Sandra (2005). *Liquid Assets: The Critical Need to Safeguard Freshwater Ecosystems*, Worldwatch Paper 170, Washington, DC: Worldwatch Institute.

Potorti, Mary (2006), "Jell-O: The Mold and Make of an American Classic," *UMBC Review* 7: 10–31.

Probyn, Elspeth (2000), *Carnal Appetites: FoodSexIdentities*, London: Routledge.

Proust, Marcel (1913, 1934), *Remembrance of Things Past*, Vol. 1, trans. C. K. Scott Moncrieff, New York: Random House.

Pullar, Philippa (1970), *Consuming Passions: A History of English Food and Appetite*, New York: Little, Brown.

Raeburn, Paul (1995), *The Last Harvest: The Genetic Gamble that Threatens to Destroy American Agriculture*, Lincoln: University of Nebraska Press.

Ray, Krishnendu (2004), *The Migrant's Table: Meals and Memories in Bengali-American Households*, Philadelphia: Temple University Press.

Reichl, Ruth (1998), *Tender at the Bone: Growing Up at the Table*, New York: Broadway Books.

Rensberger, Boyce (1991), "Anthropology: Diets that Define Amazon Tribes," *Washington Post,* December 30, p. A3.

Rhodes, Richard (1989), *Farm: A Year in the Life of an American Farmer*, New York: Simon & Schuster.

Rifkin, Jeremy (1992), *Beyond Beef: The Rise and Fall of the Cattle Culture*, New York: Plume.

Ritzer, George (1993), *The McDonaldization of Society: An Investigation into the Changing Character of Contemporary Social Life*, Thousand Oaks, CA: Pine Forge Press.

Robbins, John (1985), *Diet for a New America*, Walpole, NH: Stillpoint.

Rosin, Jacob and Eastman, Max (1953), *The Road to Abundance*, New York: McGraw-Hill.

Rosner, Lisa (ed.) (2004), *The Technological Fix: How People Use Technology to Create and Solve Problems*, New York: Routledge.

Rosofsky, Meryl S. (2004), "Writing the Wolf Away: Food Meaning and Memories from World War II," *Food, Culture and Society* 7(1), pp. 47–58.

Ross, Alice (2004), "Catherine Beecher," in Andrew Smith (ed.), *The Oxford Encyclopedia of Food and Drink in America*, New York: Oxford University Press, p. 75.

Ross, Eric B. (1987), "Theoretical Overview," in Marvin Harris and Eric B. Ross (eds), *Food and Human Evolution*, Philadelphia: Temple University Press, pp. 7–55.

Roth, LuAnne K. (2005), "'Beef. It's What's for Dinner': Vegetarians, Meat-Eaters and the Negotiation of Familial Relationships," *Food, Culture and Society* 8 (2): 181–200.

Rothenberg, Daniel (2000), *With These Hands: The Hidden World of Migrant Farmworkers Today*, Berkeley: University of California Press.

Rozanov, Boris H., Targulian, Viktor and Orlov, D. C. (1990), "Soils," in B. L. Turner et al. (eds), *The Earth as Transformed by Human Action*, Cambridge: Cambridge University Press, pp. 203–14.

Rozin, Elisabeth (1982), "The Structure of Cuisine," in Lewis M. Barker (ed.), *The Psychobiology of Human Food Selection*, Westport, CT: AVI Publishing, pp. 189–203.

Rozin, Elisabeth (1994), *The Primal Cheeseburger. A Generous Helping of Food History Served On a Bun*, New York: Penguin.

Rozin, Paul (1999), "Food is Fundamental, Fun, Frightening, and Far-Reaching," in Mack, Arien (ed.), "Food: Nature and Culture," *Social Research* 66(1), pp. 9–30.

Salaman, Redcliffe N. (1949), *The History and Social Influence of the Potato*, Cambridge: Cambridge University Press.

Sale, Kirkpatrick (1991), *The Conquest of Paradise: Christopher Columbus and the Columbian Legacy*, New York: Plume.

Sauer, Carl (1937), "Prospects for Redistribution of Population," in Isaiah Bowman (ed.), *Limits of Land Settlement*, New York: Council on Foreign Relations, pp. 14–24.

Schlosser, Eric (2001), *Fast Food Nation: The Dark Side of the All-American Meal*, Boston: Houghton-Mifflin.

Schwartz, Hillel (1986), *Never Satisfied: A Cultural History of Diets, Fantasies, and Fat*, New York: Free Press.

Schwartz-Nobel, Loretta (2002), *Growing Up Empty: How Federal Policies are Starving America's Children*, New York: Perennial.

Scully, Matthew (2002), *Dominion: The Power of Man, the Suffering of Animals, and a Call to Mercy*, New York: St Martin's Press.

Sears, Paul B. (1959), *Deserts on the March*, 3rd edn, Norman: University of Oklahoma Press.

Shapiro, Laura (1986), *Perfection Salad: Women and Cooking at the Turn of the Century*, New York: Farrar, Straus & Giroux.

Shapiro, Laura (2004), *Something from the Oven: Reinventing Dinner in 1950s America*, New York: Viking.

Shields-Argelès, Christy (2004), "Imagining the Self and the Other: Food and Identity in France and the United States," *Food, Culture and Society* 7(2): 13–28.

Sinclair, Upton (1906), *The Jungle*, New York: Doubleday, Jabber and Co.

Singer, Isaac Bashevis (1983), *The Penitent*, New York: Fawcett Crest.

Singer, Peter and Mason, Jim (2006), *The Way We Eat: Why Our Food Choices Matter*, Emmaus, PA: Rodale.

Slotnick, Bonnie (2004), "Sylvester Graham," in Andrew Smith (ed.), *Oxford Encyclopedia of Food and Drink in America*, New York: Oxford University Press, pp. 573–4.

Smil, Vaclav (2000), *Feeding the World: A Challenge for the Twenty-First Century*, Cambridge, MA: MIT Press.

Smith, Andrew F. (1994), *The Tomato in America: Early History, Culture, and Cookery*, Columbia, SC: University of South Carolina Press.

Smith, Andrew F. (2001), *Popped Culture: A Social History of Popcorn in America*, Washington, DC: Smithsonian Institution Press.

Smith, Andrew F. (2002), *Peanuts: The Illustrious History of the Goober Pea*, Urbana: University of Illinois Press.

Smith, Andrew F. (ed.) (2004), *The Oxford Encyclopedia of Food and Drink in America*, New York: Oxford University Press.

Smith, J. Russell (1919), *The World's Food Resources*, New York: Henry Holt.

Sobal, Jeffery (1999), "Food System Globalization, Eating Transformations, and Nutrition Transitions," in Raymond Grew (ed.), *Food in Global History*, Boulder, CO: Westview, pp. 171–93.

Sobal, Jeffery and Maurer, Donna (eds) (1999a), *Interpreting Weight: The Social Management of Fatness and Thinness*, New York: Aldine de Gruyter.

Sobal, Jeffery and Maurer, Donna (eds) (1999b), *Weighty Issues: Fatness and Thinness as Social Problems*, New York: Aldine de Gruyter.

Sobo, Elisa J. (1997), "The Sweetness of Fat: Health, Procreation, and Sociability in Rural Jamaica," in Carole M. Counihan and Penny Van Esterik (eds), *Food and Culture: A Reader*, New York: Routledge, pp. 256–71.

Solbrig, Otto T. and Solbrig, Dorothy J. (1994), *So Shall You Reap: Farming and Crops in Human Affairs*, Washington, DC: Island Press.

Soluri, John (2005), *Banana Cultures: Agriculture, Consumption, and Environmental Change in Honduras and the United States*, Austin: University of Texas Press.

Spencer, Colin (1995), *The Heretic's Feast: A History of Vegetarianism*, Hanover, NH: University Press of New England.

Squires, Sally (2002), "Study Finds That in US, 1 in 3 Are Obese," *Washington Post*, October 9: A18.

Starhawk (1993), *The Fifth Sacred Thing*, New York: Bantam Books.

Stearns, Peter N. (1997), *Fat History: Bodies and Beauty in the Modern West*, New York: New York University Press.

Steinberg, Ellen F. (2007), *Learning to Cook in 1898: A Chicago Culinary Memoir*, Detroit, MI: Wayne State University Press.

Stern, Jane and Stern, Michael (1984), *Square Meals*, New York: Knopf.

Stokes, Sutton (2005), "'The Right Thing to Do': Taking a Closer Look at Quaker Oats," *Food, Culture and Society* 8(1): 73–95.

Stoll, Steven (1998), *The Fruits of Natural Advantage. Making the Industrial Countryside in California*, Berkeley: University of California Press.

Strasser, Susan (1982), *Never Done: A History of American Housework*, New York: Pantheon Books.

Sutton, David E. (2001), *Remembrance of Repasts: An Anthropology of Food and Memory*, Oxford: Berg.

Theophano, Janet (2002), *Eat My Words: Reading Women's Lives through the Cookbooks They Wrote*, New York: Palgrave.

Tobias, Ruth (2004), "Toast," in Andrew Smith (ed.), *Oxford Encyclopedia of Food and Drink in America*, New York: Oxford University Press, p. 122.

Tompkins, Kyla Wazana (2005), "Literary Approaches to Food Studies: Eating the Other," *Food, Culture and Society* 8(2): 243–58.

Tribe, Derek (1994), *Feeding and Greening the World: The Role of International Agricultural Research*, Oxford: CAB International.

Tuchman, Gaye and Levine, Harry Gene (1993), "New York Jews and Chinese Food: The Social Construction of an Ethnic Pattern," reprinted in Barbara G. Shortridge and James R. Shortridge (eds), *The Taste of American Place: A Reader on Regional and Ethnic Foods*, Lanham, MD: Rowman & Littlefield, 1998, pp. 163–84.

Turner, Katherine Leonard (2006), "Buying, Not Cooking: Ready-to-eat Food in American Urban Working-Class Neighborhoods, 1880–1930," *Food, Culture and Society* 9(1): 13–40.

Visser, Margaret (1986), *Much Depends on Dinner*, New York: Collier.

Visser, Margaret (1991), *The Rituals of Dinner: The Origins, Evolution, Eccentricities, and Meaning of Table* Manners, New York: Grove Weidenfeld.

Visser, Margaret (2003), "Etiquette and Eating Habits," in Solomon Katz (ed.), *Encyclopedia of Food and Culture*, New York: Scribner's, pp. 586–92.

Vogt, William (1948), *The Road to Survival*, New York: William Sloane Associates.

Wackernagel, Mathis and Rees, William (1996), *Our Ecological Footprint: Reducing Human Impact on the Earth,* Gabriola Island, BC: New Society Publishers.

Waggoner, Paul E. (1994), *How Much Land Can Ten Billion People Spare for Nature?* Task Force Report 121 (February), Ames, IA: Council for Agricultural Science and Technology.

Walters, Kerry S. and Portmess, Lisa (eds) (1999), *Ethical Vegetarianism: From Pythagoras to Peter Singer*, Albany, NY: State University of New York Press.

Wansink, Brian, and Cynthia Sangerman (2000), "The Taste of Comfort: Food for Thought on How Americans Eat to Feel Better," *American Demographics* 22(7): 66–7.

Wansink, Brian (2006), *Mindless Eating: Why We Eat More Than We Think*, New York: Bantam.

Warshall, Peter (2002), "Tilth and Technology: The Industrial Redesign of Our Nation's Soils," in Andrew Kimbrell (ed.), *The Fatal Harvest Reader: The Tragedy of Industrial Agriculture*, Washington, DC: Island Press, pp. 167–80.

Watson, James L. (ed.) (1997), *Golden Arches East: McDonald's in East Asia*, Palo Alto, CA: Stanford University Press.

Watson, James L. and Caldwell, Melissa L. (eds) (2005), *The Cultural Politics of Eating: A Reader*, Oxford: Blackwell.

Weir, David, and Shapiro, Mark (1981), *The Circle of Poison*, San Francisco: Institute for Food and Development Policy.

West, Michael Lee (2000), *Consuming Passions: A Food-Obsessed Life*, New York: HarperCollins.

Whorton, James C. (1982), *Crusaders for Fitness: The History of American Health Reformers*, Princeton, NJ: Princeton University Press.

Wilk, Richard R. (2002), "Food and Nationalism: The Origins of 'Belizean Food,'" in Warren Belasco and Philip Scranton (eds), *Food Nations: Selling Taste in Consumer Societies*, New York: Routledge, pp. 67–89.

Wilk, Richard (2006), *Home Cooking in the Global Village: Caribbean Food From Buccaneers to Ecotourists*, Oxford: Berg Publishers.

Wilkins, Jennifer (2005), "Seeing Beyond the Package. Teaching About the Food System through Food Product Analysis," *Food, Culture and Society* 8(1): 97–114.

Williams, Brett (1984), "Why Migrant Women Feed Their Husbands Tamales: Foodways as a Basis for as Revisionist View of Tejano Family Life," in Linda Keller Brown and Kay Mussell (eds), *Ethnic and Regional Foodways in the United States: The Performance of Group Identity*, Knoxville, TN: University of Tennessee Press, pp. 113–26.

Williams-Forson, Psyche A. (2006), *Building Houses Out of Chicken Legs: Black Women, Food, and Power*, Chapel Hill, NC: University of North Carolina Press.

Williamson, Judith (1985), *Consuming Passions*, London: Marion Boyars.

Wilson, C. Anne (1999), *The Book of Marmalade*, Philadelphia: University of Pennsylvania Press.

Winegardner, Mark (ed.) (1998), *We Are What We Ate: Twenty-Four Memories of Food*, New York: Harcourt Brace & Co.

Worster, Donald (1979), *Dust Bowl: The Southern Plains in the 1930s*, New York: Oxford University Press.

Worster, Donald (1985), *Rivers of Empire: Water, Aridity, and the Growth of the American West*, New York: Pantheon Books.

Wright, Angus (1990), *The Death of Ramon Gonzalez: The Modern Agricultural Dilemma*, Austin: University of Texas Press.

Wu, David Y. H. (1997), "McDonald's in Taipei: Hamburgers, Betel Nuts, and National Identity," in James L. Watson (ed.), *Golden Arches East: McDonald's in East Asia*, Palo Alto, CA: Stanford University Press, pp. 110–35.

Yan, Yunxiang (1997), "McDonald's in Beijing: The Localization of Americana," in James L. Watson (ed.), *Golden Arches East: McDonald's in East Asia*, Palo Alto, CA: Stanford University Press, pp. 39–76.

Young, Carolyn C. (2004), "Silverware," in Andrew Smith (ed.), *Oxford Encyclopedia of Food and Drink in America*, New York: Oxford University Press, pp. 432–38.

INDEX